MW01092130

Kali Rising: Holy Rage

Girl God Books

Edited by C. Ara Campbell,
Jaclyn Cherie, Pat Daly,
and Trista Hendren

Cover Art by Kat Shaw

©2024 All Rights Reserved
ISBN: 978-82-93725-42-8

www.thegirlgod.com

Praise for Kali Rising: Holy Rage

"These are the days when a rage most righteous is a lantern we carry, a holy flame we trust will illuminate the hidden way forward as we continue this global Underworld journey. Here, as we walk together through the dark, we spit curses at the war-mongers, sing over the shattered bones of our broken beliefs, and hear the howls of mothers echo through the caverns of deep time. Here, in this haunted forest thick with all the old ghosts, we need poetry full of teeth and awe. We need prayers for peace, yes, but also for justice and truth, and we need to sense the unseen intelligence afoot. To that end, *Kali Rising* is an epic and timely achievement, another vital resource from Girl God Books for those who walk the otherworldly road." -Danielle Dulsky, founder of The Hag School and author of *Bones & Honey, The Holy Wild*, and *Sacred Hags Oracle*

"*Kali Rising: Holy Rage* masterfully weaves a tapestry of stories of fierce resilience. Every chapter immerses the reader in a world where strength is found in the untamed parts of ourselves and rage is a catalyst for profound change. This collection of stories is a testament to the collective wisdom, vulnerability and creativity that arises when women unite to speak their truth about the potency of holy rage and resilience." -Shann Vander Leek, Transformation Goddess

"A diverse group of women from around the world has come together to create this offering to Kali and women everywhere. Each of the 41 contributors shares her own unique and powerful understanding of Kali—some in words, some in art—helping the reader to forge her own relationship with this transforming warrior Goddess."
-Kim Wilborn, goddesstelesummit.com

"Power, pain, and rage are the themes of this book, but not in the way you might imagine! No longer are these to be feared by women who have been made silent, painted as soft and meek, made less. We are silent no longer! *Kali Rising: Holy Rage* encourages us to scream our truth and find the power we all hold within, no matter what that looks like, providing unique and varied perspectives into this often misunderstood goddess. This is a must-read for anyone seeking to find their own untamed, untethered truth."
-Emma Kathryn, Author of *Season Songs: Rediscovering the Magic in the Cycles of Nature*

Girl God Books

Re-visioning Medusa: from Monster to Divine Wisdom

A remarkable collection of essays, poems, and art by scholars who have researched Her, artists who have envisioned Her, and women who have known Her in their personal story. All have spoken with Her and share something of their communion in this anthology.

Inanna's Ascent: Reclaiming Female Power

Inanna's Ascent examines how females can rise from the underworld and reclaim their power, sovereignly expressed through poetry, prose and visual art. All contributors are extraordinary women in their own right, who have been through some difficult life lessons—and are brave enough to share their stories.

Women's Sovereignty and Body Autonomy Beyond Roe v. Wade

addresses the concerns and opinions of women from around the planet. Through art and poetry, prose and personal accounts, this shared atrocity that continues to be forced on women is brought into a new light with a rebel resolve that screams "NO MORE"!

Original Resistance: Reclaiming Lilith, Reclaiming Ourselves

This anthology—a chorus of voices hitting chords of defiance, liberation, anger and joy—reclaims the goodness of women bold enough to hold tight to their essence. Through poetry, prose, incantation, prayer and imagery, women from all walks of life invite you to join them in the revolutionary act of claiming their place—of reclaiming themselves.

Warrior Queen: Answering the Call of The Morrigan

Each contributor brings The Morrigan to life with unique stories that invite readers to partake and inspire them to pen their own. Included are essays, poems, stories, chants, rituals, and art from dozens of story-tellers and artists from around the world, illustrating and recounting the many ways this powerful Goddess of war, death, and prophecy has changed their lives.

In Defiance of Oppression – The Legacy of Boudicca

An anthology that encapsulates the Spirit of the defiant warrior in a modern apathetic age. No longer will the voices of our sisters go unheard, as the ancient Goddesses return to the battlements, calling to ignite the spark within each and every one of us—to defy oppression wherever we find it, and stand together in solidarity.

On the Wings of Isis: Reclaiming the Sovereignty of Auset

For centuries, women have lived, fought and died for their equality, independence and sovereignty. Originally known as Auset, the Egyptian Goddess Isis reveals such a path. Unfurl your wings and join an array of strong women who have embodied the *Goddess of Ten Thousand Names* to celebrate their authentic selves.

The Crone Initiation*: Women Speak on the Menopause Journey

The Crone Initiation and Invitation is an anthology of women's experiences of perimenopause and menopause, and the part Goddess plays in this journey. Crone's presence in the breakdowns and breakthroughs, the disintegration and rebuilding, is expressed through words and art. Meaning is reclaimed and the power of the Elder restored.

Mentorship with Goddess: Growing Sacred Womanhood

A Sacred Woman reclaims herself as Goddess – a unique strand, frequency and incarnation of her – essential for the completion and wholeness of the spectrum of the collective Feminine. Our bodies are the gateway to recalling this truth. Mentorship with Goddess is a workbook – a year-long curriculum and programme – a rite of passage – especially useful for the transition into autonomous adulthood – the process of individuation - and then also for the menopause journey.

The Girl God

A book for children young and old, celebrating the Divine Female by Trista Hendren. Magically illustrated by Elisabeth Slettnes with quotes from various faith traditions and feminist thinkers.

Dedication:

To all Women who have had their Holy Rage silenced.
We scream in honor of you.

In remembrance of our beloved sister and fellow contributor
Barbara O'Meara.

(April 11th, 1963 – October 5th, 2023)

Rest in Power and in Peace.

We love you, Barbara.

Photo by Marta Faye Photography, "The Veil is Thin." 2020.

"Divine rage is fierce, disciplined, and visionary....
The aim of divine rage is not vengeance but to reorder the world.
It is precise and purposeful, like the focused fury projected into
the world from the forehead of the Goddess.
It points us to the humanity of even those who we were fighting....
Perhaps our task as human beings is to find safe containers for
our raw reactionary rage—and then choose to harness
that energy in a way that creates a new world for all of us."

-Valarie Kaur, *See No Stranger*

Table of Contents

Answering Kali's Call

Jaclyn Cherie

Kali (Kala or Kaali).

Kali Ka (Kaalika).

Kali Ma (Kali Mata or Kaali Maa).

Chaturbhuja Kali.

Chinnamasta.

Kaushika.

The Black One.

Beyond Time.

She Who is Death.

The Dark Mother.

Kali is a Goddess of many forms, names, and energies.
To some She embodies Shakti energy.

In Shakti and Tantric Beliefs, She is worshipped as the ultimate reality or Brahman; the Highest Principal energy.

In this form, She is the first Principal energy known of Adi Shakti (Adi Parashakti, Abhya Shakti, Devi or Mahadevi: The Supreme Goddess).

Her origin story depends greatly upon which Hindu tradition one subscribes to.

Hindu Goddesses are believed to come from one singular Divine Energy, Cosmic Mother, and/or Supreme Goddess.

We can compare this to Para Brahman when dealing with Hindu Gods, Brahma the Creator, Vishnu the Preserver, Shiva the Destroyer. Singular Gods that came from one Divine Manifestation of God.

I am Shaivite Hindu, and thus I believe this Great Goddess to be Parvati, Durga, Lalita, and Kali.

Shaktism believes in Durga, Tripura Sundari, Bhuvaneshvari, and Kali.

Vaishnavism believes in Lakshmi.

This is barely skimming the surface of Her origins. They are layered, complex and overlap in many places.

When we look at Her story of Origin, we are looking at Ancient Texts such as: Devi Mahatmyam, Linga Purana, and the Vamana Purana.

In Devi Mahatmyam, it is said that Mahakali appears from Vishnu's sleeping body to wake him up to protect the world from two asuras (demons). Mahakali takes the form of Mahamaya and enchants the demons allowing Vishnu to kill them.

Later in the story, Durga is attacked by the same two demons, Chanda and Munda, this enrages Durga so much that Kali emerges from Her forehead. When faced with a formidable demon named Raktabija, who can perpetually regenerate, Kali sucks/drains his blood and eats each of his regenerated forms. In this text Kali is known as, "Durga's wrath, and fury personified."

The Linga Purana, however, describes Her story of Origin as, Shiva asking Parvati to defeat an asura named Daruka, who can only be killed by a Woman. Parvati merges with Shiva, and then Kali emerges.

She defeats Daruka and Her thirst for blood becomes insatiable. This is where we see Shiva stepping in and lying beneath Kali's feet. He was the only thing that could stop Her rage. As the Destroyer, Shiva can be destroyed and created again.

The Vamana Purana tells a different tale and one that can explain a lot of colorism that occurs within India and that has occurred for centuries. In this text, Parvati merges with Shiva to create Kali, however, when Parvati recognizes that She is being addressed as "the dark blue one" or "the black one" by Shiva, She becomes embarrassed. This is where some of the translations, or at least schools of thought, that Kali's tongue is not one of rage but of humility come from. She was so embarrassed by Her actions that only Shiva could stop Her so She bears Her tongue to show respect, meekness, and submission.

Parvati so offended lightens Her complexion to become Gauri, the Golden One. Her Dark shedding becomes Kausiki who, deeply offended by Parvati, becomes enraged and creates Kali, as a standalone Goddess.

Regardless of which Origin story you subscribe to, Kali was necessary to defeat evil and save the world.

So, how, exactly has She found Her way into modern pop culture, Witchcraft, and Feminism?

Women and Femmes answered Her call.

That's how.

She is rage and wrath embodied.

Are Women and Femmes not angry as fuck?

Are we not valid in our anger?

In tumultuous times we turn to energies, deities, and mythos that we can relate to; Kali is one of those stories, one of those energies.

She has been watered down a lot in Western Culture and in some cases totally removed from Her Indian roots. This is where Cultural Appropriation vs Cultural Appreciation can really be seen.

Kali is known to destroy the bad, then She destroys the good, and finally She destroys Herself or Ego because not even She exists, and then the cycle starts again. This too will be what happens to you, your life, and your Ego if you decide to accept Her call.

Kali is not for the faint hearted, She is not a nurturing Mother, She is fierce.

She is justified rage EMBODIED.

This word cannot be stressed enough: Embodied.

When we are fighting back against oppression of all forms from racism, sexism, colorism, to ableism, and more, our best ally, our strongest tool is justified rage.

Justified rage is what clears the path for the new to be built.

It is what burns old systems to the ground so that we can RISE from the ashes.

Justified rage is a weapon gifted to us by Divinity.

This book and the books in this series to follow will tell the tales of how Kali changed, shaped, and molded the lives of Women and Femmes.

This collection is potent. You will be left crying while screaming "FUCK YES!"

This book is a testament to what happens when you answer Kali's call, and how transformative it can be.

When we control our rage, hone our rage, and use our rage we become united with the Divine and we are unstoppable.

Rage is Sacred.

Rage is Holy.

And so is this book.

Sacred Rage

Kat Shaw

About this Anthology

Trista Hendren

Kali Rising: Holy Rage contains a variety of writing styles from around the world. Several forms of English are included in this anthology, and we chose to keep spellings of the writers' place of origin to honor/honour everyone's unique voice.

It was the express intent of the editors to not police standards of citation, transliteration, and formatting. Contributors have determined which citation style, italicization policy and transliteration system to adopt in their pieces. The resulting diversity reflects the diverse academic fields, genres and personal expressions represented by the authors.[1]

As we began to put together this collection, I was bombarded by people on Facebook who were upset about it. The argument was generally that Kali has Hindu origins, and I should not be writing in ways that challenge (what I consider to be) the patriarchal understanding of Her.

I do not claim to fully understand a tradition with over a billion adherents—and vast interpretations of it. I am not a Hindu, so I will save those talking points for those who know the religion best.

What I do know from studying early divinities is that Kali was with us long before any of the male gods.

> "In the world's oldest creation myths, the female god creates the world out of her own body. The Great Mother everywhere was the active and autonomous creatrix of the

---

[1] This paragraph is borrowed and adapted with love from *A Jihad for Justice: Honoring the Work and Life of Amina Wadud.* Edited by Kecia Ali, Juliane Hammer and Laury Silvers.

world . . . and, unlike the aloof and self-righteous patriarchal gods who only recently usurped her mountain-throne, the ancient Goddess was always there—alive, immanent—within her creation; no ontological scapegoater, she was wholly responsible for both the pain and the good of life."[2]

Several people also threatened me over Kali's nakedness on the front cover of this book. This was intentional.

"The nudity of the goddess is not an anomaly…. Evidence of other nude goddess figures from other parts of India starting from 2500 BCE confirms that nudity was equated with the fertility of goddesses for many centuries."[3]

It has been my observation that as patriarchy took hold, women—and their deities—were more and more covered up. Kali is no exception.

As Carol P. Christ noted:

"Visual images of the Goddesses stand in stark contrast to the image of God as an old white man, jarring us to question our culture's view that all legitimate power is male, and that female power is dangerous and evil. The image of the naked Eve brazenly taking the apple from the serpent, then cowering in shame before a wrathful male God, tells us not only that female will is the source of all the evil in the universe, but also that the naked female body is part of the problem. This image communicates to the deep mind the message that female will and female nakedness must be controlled and punished by male authority. In contrast, the Goddesses show us that the

[2] Sjöö, Monica and Mor, Barbara. *The Great Cosmic Mother: Rediscovering the Religion of the Earth*. HarperOne; 2nd edition, 1987).
[3] Padma, Sree. *Vicissitudes of the Goddess: Reconstructions of the Gramadevata in India's Religious Traditions*. Oxford University Press; 2013.

female can be symbolic of all that is creative and powerful in the universe. The simplest and most profound meaning of the image of the Goddess is the legitimacy and goodness of female power, the female body, and female will."[4]

There is power in female nudity. There is no hiding where life comes from and who nourishes it.

It makes me furious that we are still being told what to write (don't rock the boat), how to act (not angry), and how to dress (cover it up!)—even by other women!

The time for patriarchal control over what women do—religious or otherwise—is over. We must control our own narratives. This anthology is a starting point.

Each contributor is on a different part of her journey. The beauty of anthologies is the variety of perspectives they can hold within one book.

We welcome you to join us in the circle of women who have shared art or writing in this book—as we learn to claim our holy rage.

If you find that a particular writing doesn't sit well with you, please feel free to use the Al-Anon suggestion: "Take what you like, leave the rest!" That said, if there aren't at least several pieces that challenge you, we have not done our job here.

---

[4] Christ, Carol P. *Rebirth Of The Goddess: Finding Meaning In Feminist Spirituality.* Da Capo Press; 1997.

Goddess Kali

Andrea Ayla Sib

Battle Cry

C. Ara Campbell

Kali, Destroyer of Obstacles, we hear your fierce roar. As you once freed the land by consuming unconquerable demons, we call upon you, Great Devourer, to stand with us and reclaim the world from the grip of the vile forces that would subjugate it.
We raise our blades with you, bloody but unbowed. We shall not yield. We shall not forgive those who continue to forcefully trespass against us. Your courage burns like fire in our veins, your ancient wisdom emblazed upon our hearts.

Walk with us as we avenge the persecuted and purge the poison of the toxic patriarchal system that would see us enslaved. Breathing holy wildfire, raze the false corporate gods who do the bidding of the elite to the ground. Feast upon their treacherous souls in a frenzy of fury, your vengeance swift and terrible.

Black Goddess of Transformation, guide us as we burn away false illusions and rise from the ashes of the old paradigms to create our world anew. We rage, Kali, crying out for revolution. In defiance, we rebel against their chains. We will never again be sacrificed upon their altars. We take back our bones, our spirits, and our truth, rising together to vanquish the oppressors.

We are the wild untamed beings that refuse to back down or give up. We are your soldiers, fighting for the freedom of all. Your howl is our battle cry, feral and raw. For you are the winds of change that sweep the land. And we ride fiercely by your side.

Kali – Dark Mother, Dark Goddess

Shalini Angela Persaud

Kali is one of the most well-known Hindu goddesses who is also known as Kālikā and is associated with empowerment or *shakti*. Goddess Kali is a Tamil goddess and the dark manifestation of the Hindu Goddess Durga (who is regarded as the Divine Mother, the Mother Goddess, and the mother of the universe) Kali in turn, is the fearful, ferocious, and powerful form of Durga. The name Kali comes from the word *kāla*, which means black, time, death.

Many regard Kali as a goddess of death and destruction, but the death referred to is not the actual physical death but rather, the death of the ego as our illusory concept of reality. The worship and reverence of Goddess Kali allows us to see the reality behind the illusion. Goddess Kali destroys solely to recreate, and what she destroys is ignorance, deception, and decay. In honouring this dark deity, she transforms you and changes you from within so that what was once a priority in life no longer is because it no longer holds any importance or value to you.

Kali is equated with the eternal night, the darkness from which everything was created. She is the transcendent power of time, creation and destruction and is the consort of the Hindu god Shiva. Therefore, Kali is Shiva's *shakti*, the primal energy which accompanies Shiva's consciousness.

A tantric interpretation sees Shiva as consciousness and Kali as power or energy. Consciousness and energy are dependent upon each other, since Shiva depends on *shakti*, or energy, to fulfill his role in creation, preservation, and destruction.

Kali receives her name because she devours *kala* (time) and then resumes her own dark formlessness. Kali literally means *"The Black One"*. She is the power of time which devours all. She has a power that destroys and is regarded in awe-inspiring terror. As the limitless Void, Kali has swallowed up everything without a trace and since the colour black absorbs everything, Kali is thus black.

Physical Appearance and Symbolism

Kali's fierce physical form is rich in symbolism. Her black complexion symbolizes her all-embracing and transcendental nature. Kali is portrayed mostly in two forms: the popular four-armed form or the ten-armed *Mahakali* form.

In both of her forms, she is described as being black in colour but is most often depicted as blue in popular Indian art. Kali's most common four-armed image shows each hand carrying a sword, a trident, a severed head, and a bowl catching the blood of the severed head. The sword signifies divine knowledge through the destruction of false consciousness, and the human head symbolizes human ego, which must be symbolically "slain" by this divine knowledge. The trident and the bowl symbolize fearlessness and blessings/boons granted to those who revere her with a true heart. She has a garland consisting of fifty human heads, which represent the fifty letters of the Sanskrit alphabet. Hindus believe Sanskrit is a language of dynamism, and each of these letters represents a form of energy, or a form of Kali. Her girdle of severed human hands signifies work and liberation from the cycle of karma.

Her tongue protrudes from her mouth, her eyes are red, and she stands with one foot on the ground, and another on the chest of her husband, Shiva. Her proximity to cremation grounds symbolizes the death of worldly attachments and the birth of new spirituality, hence the eternal cycle of birth and death.

My Relationship with the Dark Mother

There were no messages in dreams or visions or calling. I had a severe problem at work and I had the strongest feeling to go and find Kali in a temple and tell her all about it. I was not brought up as a Hindu or as a spiritual person. I was Catholic... yet I blindly went in search of Kali Ma. And on reaching the temple, the pujari (Hindu priest) said to me that he was expecting me. He then guided me to the 6-foot murti of Kali... and I rang the bell before her, and told her all my problems. For 4 hours. Time was a haze. I had no idea that I was crying, I had no idea what time it was. I just had the blind faith in the fact that this strong, powerful warrior goddess would make it all right, avenge my cause and defend me from all negative energies. And she did. And I will always be eternally in her debt. And that was my first meeting with Kali Ma.

I prepared an altar for her at home in gratitude, and from then on, I have honoured and loved Kali Ma as my first Shakti goddess and my most special. We share a love like no other. She has helped me to be a better person – more self-disciplined, emotionally and mentally stronger and resilient against all the negativity of life. She has always given hope, courage, guidance, and love.

Kali creates and nourishes our spirituality just as she kills and destroys our ego. She is *shakti* (female energy) incarnate and the manifestation of primordial power. She enters our darkness and radically transforms our lives by showing us how to embrace that which is dark within us. All we have to do is to surrender to her fully and allow her to cleanse, transform and recreate.

To honour Kali Ma, you must be true, authentic, real, humble. She asks that you love her and believe in her, and in return, she will protect you as well as throw you into the abyss to learn lessons which will make you spiritually stronger, resilient, invincible, and disciplined. She is the Warrior, the Mother, the Protector, and she will never let you down or be false.

Kali of the Seer
Kat Shaw

Kali: Sacred Rage

Tamara Albanna

I found Kali, or rather she found me, during the siege of Daesh on Mosel in 2014. It's been almost ten years since, the genocide of the Yazidis. The world watched and did nothing while women and girls were enslaved, raped, and murdered. A scene that has played out time and again throughout our history. Women and girls endlessly on the frontlines of male violence. It was as though nothing had changed, and we were just expected to watch yet another atrocity unfold, with no recourse.

It was Kali the Destroyer, the one with sacred rage. She was the only one I could feel during that time, when things were so hopeless, when anger was on the surface and the patriarchy marched on raping and murdering with impunity. It's cyclical. History, the violence, the never-ending killing machine of armed men, whether by terrorist organization or government, the outcome always the same. Complete destruction. The world eventually forgets, until the next time, and there's always a next time. It's always women at the forefront of this violence.

Kali was born on the battlefield according to her origin story. She is the direct result of war, a response to it. I am far from being an authority on Kali, but it seems to me that as the Dark Mother, she is destroyer of worlds, but she also creates. She is then, in my eyes, a response to the murdering patriarchy. She is the perfect symbol of cleansing with fire. Her fire being her rage and justice. Justice for the long-suffering women and girls all over the world.

The war machine rages on, and we are once again confronted with horrific acts of violence. Again, the male who sees himself as god, decides who lives and who dies. In times of horror we have often heard, "Where is God?" Well, my response to that is, "She's right here." Within all of us, within our hearts. Kali is a force that predates tradition. When Matriarchy was overthrown, the Dark

Mother emerged to avenge her children. Just as she emerges every time history repeats. She never left, but we may have forgotten Her.

It is not the gentle loving mother we need, but the destroyer. It is the only way we will ever have a chance to save our planet from the killing machines and the men who operate them.

Patriarchy is anti-human; the Goddess is life. No matter what form she takes. Right now, we need all her fire – and her sacred rage.

The Dance of Kali

Nuit Moore

The Dance of Kali

Nuit Moore

Jai Maa, Jai Kali Maa, Jai Maa Durga, Springing Forth the Form!
Benevolent One, Merciful One, Compassionate One!
The Dance of Kali is unfolding,
and I have faith where Her feet will land.
She is dancing the Towers of Oppression down-
they are coming down.
Lightning bolt, shattering the foundation,
crumbling the obelisk, with howls of rage.
She is swiftly revealing truth,
the Veils of Illusion, they disintegrate.
The light has been turned on,
and the degeneration is being shown to us.
The malignancies are shown,
and the time is NOW for the major battle.
The annihilation of imprisoning paradigms.
The annihilation of the illusions of division.
The annihilation of systems of oppression and injustice.
This is a catalyst- the manifestation of true revolution.
Queen of Regeneration, do the work, through us, we do the work.
We are each a lotus blooming, refusing the refuse.

Maa Kali is manifesting on high in this here and now,
the energy of the Destroyer/Creator,
Beloved Dark Mother, saying REMEMBER.
Remember the Holy in All things; Life and Death, the Womb and
the Tomb, the Void and the Fullness, the White Light and the
Blackest Darkness, the Sun that eats dreams and the Moon that
makes them, the split-second lightning dance between the
in-breath and the out-breath-for All are One.
All spin as One in the Abyss of Her Womb.
All touch the Veil.
All Receive the Ebb and the Flow.

The Sprout of the Blood-thick Root, and the Bones in the Decay.
When Kali cuts us down with Her Sword of Justice and Mercy,
it is the Release and the Liberation,
it is the Ending and the Beginning.
And She is here NOW.

As Ramprasad Sen has said:
'Meditate on Kali! Why be anxious?

The night of delusion is over; it's almost dawn.'
Yes, the Dance of Kali is unfolding,
and I have faith in where Her feet will land.
Bring it down, bring it down, bring it down, Dark Mother.
Dance with on the Bones of what must be transformed.
Jai Maa!

Kali-Durga
Juliana Garces

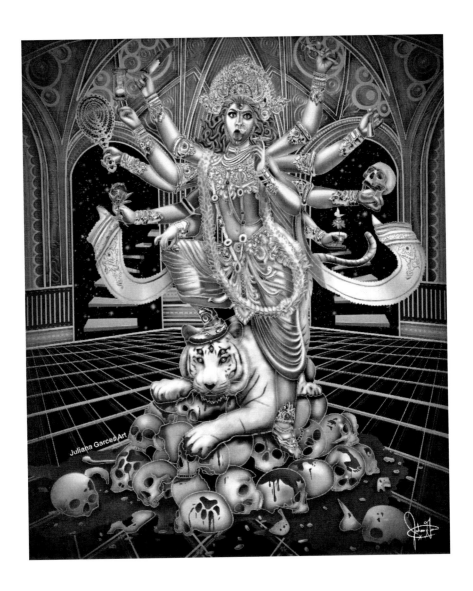

In Her Name

Jen Abha

I awake, and call out to you – in my pain, suffering, avoidance, ignorance, anguish, anger, holy rage...

At the injustices of my own personal hurts and the collective, long overdue, and ancient suffering of the modern age.

Sensing the fire deep in the core of my belly, trickling down to my toes, shooting up to my mind, alive in my heart, my precious, beloved, holy womb.

I sense your fervent ever-present fury alive and well in my movement, my breath – in all my sensing, knowing, intuiting, like the tides of the moon.

The unraveling of the jagged edges that have tried... oh so hard, to take root in my glorious temple.

Yet through channeling the light, and essence of your very reverent goddess self leaves me–
Pregnant and full.

Of the promise of our precious future through the steadfast courage of those priestess souls committing to connect deep within.

Honoring moments to hold the sacred grief, death, sorrow, losses, and pain accepting nobly where we have been.

Ushering in tiny ripples and tidal waves of authenticity.

For how we all seek to connect, reflect, pause and Be.

For the holy union of the divine feminine and holy masculine occurs in our beings.

When we lay our brave offerings at your feet trusting the holy rage will provide us our wings.

Wings of connected weblike strength that intertwine our sensitive and strong universal Power.

We create, thrive, die and destruct as living embodiments of the Tower.

Intending to grow – grow well beyond this static existence of duality.

Avidya cast aside as we step into the dynamism of the divine here, we are intended to clearly see.

Allowing and circulating the blessed rage, fury, passion, while fire and puja mold us like a striking hot skewer.

Piercing all obstacles cast around from ego world that attempts to cloak the light in pervasive and perpetual fear—

We pray infinitely to engage your energy, love light, essence, dear Kali—

For a bright and vibrant future overflowing with love and justice
for me,
and mine,
and yours,
and all who truly believe
in embracing the divine feminine.

Knowing rage and anger serve as catalysts for all that has ever been.

Oppressing, and serving as punishment reinforcing status quo.

Trusting the awake will soon rise for all—
The world to embrace, see and know.

That your energies, dear Kali Ma, are alive, well, and serve as a bedrock.

Like a magical crystal key to the universal heart that has been fast asleep and locked.

We always remember to invoke your name, dear Kali, as a source of strength and inspiration.

We commit to rely on intention, compassion, and persistence in the process of phoenixing.

We give thanks, blessings and gratitude as we lay our offerings on the altar, trusting in you, as together we Sing
Your holy name.

Dear Goddess, your compassion envelopes us all in a cloak of holy protective light-filled and radiant armor, empowering us to grow well beyond our perceived limitations, listening deeply to the seed of love within, that is always present on our journey of this earthly existence while inviting in the heavenly realms of divinity with the sincere utmost reverence.

For the journey each of us walks in our own sacred way, each as part of the whole, the interconnected tapestry the parts and wholeness of our stories weave together as part of the greater mystery.

May together parts of our humanity die, with the prayerful support of you Kali, so that we may be reborn a more compassionate, loving, intentional version of our Higher Selves.

Together.
In Her Name.

Sat Nam.

Authentic Self

Sonee Singh

Oh Kali, exalted one
How you break me
Crack me open
I shed darkness
Density and weight
Break away the shackles
Feel freedom and ease
Walking in my own skin
Myself at home
In chaos and disruption
Pupa emerging
Shedding the cocoon
The old dies
The new rises
More me than before
Beautiful and magnificent
Rising from the fray
A quilt of patches
Oh Kali, thank you
For showing me how
To be my authentic self

*This poem was first published in Sonee's poetry book: *Embody.*

I Shall Always, Under Your Cauldron, Be the Fire

Lily Munroe

I was young, naive, and bearing pain when Kali first came –
pulsating, vivid, wearing blood like war paint, human skulls as her
necklace. She writhed in her heat, like living flesh from inside me,
calling from a void between time and space, as I stood wide-eyed,
awe-struck, mystified. She was familiar yet novel to me all at once,
while instilling a knowing that her power was vast, not fearsome;
never fearsome to the daughters she calls back to her heart.

Blessed Kali – so certain and wild to the young woman I was, long
scolded if I walked in my truth, if I shone too bright, long
ostracized, pummelled down to size, reprimanded, to dim that
light. And when your heart is big and your worth is ephemeral you
think this must be right, so you wither yourself for others to shine,
only later realising the depths of this crime.

Blessed Kali – so certain and wild to me, even though I had sought
trails with wolves, traversing with hair matted and bare-footed,
fossicking for my untamed self through forests and caves, as I
broke from the shell conformity had bred, or was that bled? Her
potency, her depths, felt too unruly for me, too powerful, too free,
so I admired while bowing my head and recoiling respectfully.
Only occasionally raising my eyes to meet the image she painted
for me. Only meeting the grand force of her embodiment when
boldness unrestrained me.

Years passed as I gained strength after strength, amid heartache
and body-break, triumph after weary triumph, with some
expecting me to fall in their wake, at times even I. And at each
ebb and flow of black and gold, I would sense her shimmering
blue, her vibration, her vigour from earth and cosmos entwined,
centred inside me, sliding through my blood, calling the primal
part of me to regenerate. Even when fog encased my forward
motion, or abandonment stole worthiness like thieves do, I felt

her pull, to get up, to shake it off, to slam that door and create anew.

I had survived – my journey tattooed across my body, some by scars, some with ink. More than survived, I had retrieved my crown from the underworld amid strewn bones – mostly my own – from battlefields with self, with self-image, with men, with peers, with family, society, dogmas, stigmas, with expectations and violations, with the history etched inside of me. Competing against opposition for my birthright, of dignity, value, liberty. Finally winning my own vision, of warrior, of witch, of rebel woman, of wisdom-seeker, of oracle, of divinities daughter, of beloved one, of creator/destroyer, all slithering within, where it had always been, now able to flourish as was written when I was born.

Kali's visitations are visceral now, animated before me, filling the space around me, through me, adored by me. Invoking ancient codes like old movies, as I dote with love and bestow gratitude upon her. My remembering, returning, becoming, aided by this primordial mother, from so many death beds and birthing circles, as I formed and shaped my own version of me, not what others wanted me to be.

Two decades on from our first blood and bone encounter of raw energetic life standing before one another, I look over the view from this midpoint of life and see so much that thrives, vibrant as the sky, as I conjure more blessings on this spinning wheel of my life, with my will, my heart, my gesturing hands, with purposeful joy as alignment's thread.

And like the blissful swell of a lover's embrace, a friend's co-merriment at your valour and fate, a faery's wand guiding the next metamorphosis, she leans close as I appreciate my healing and achievements, whispering in my ear like a warm lullaby. 'I've been with you with love all along, dear one. You only feared my power back when because you feared life. You feared truly knowing and owning yourself, because you were raised to wane rather than to run wild – the curse of the girl child.

'It was I who sealed those doors that nearly stole you away, and the portals you clung to because it was all that you knew. It was I who granted access to other ways, other phases, other stages for you to play upon. It was I who devoured the pain, the aching, the rage, when you thought the dams were going to burst in your psyche and flood you away.

'Just as it is I still, forever by your side, wild and free, a reflection of thee, my holy child now grown woman divine. So, keep rising, keep claiming your majesty. Keep serving with your magic and begin to receive, all the good you deserve, all the good you desire, as you give of the gifts from your holy empire.

'And remember me again in the next life, dear one, as you have each and every time. For this journey of a thousand lives will one day begin again, and as always, I shall, under your cauldron, be the fire.'

SHE

Jaclyn Cherie

SHE

Whose rage is insatiable
Divine, drunken bloodlust

SHE

Who is The Beginning
&
The End

SHE

Who destroys all
Creating Life from Death
&
Death from Life

SHE

Embodied Rage
Wrath Personified

SHE

Who
Saved
The
World

SHE
Whose every step
Moves
Mountains
Elements
&
Tides

SHE

The Dark Divine Feminine
Unapologetically
Wholly
Holy
Kali

SHE

Where Does This Rage Come From?

Trista Hendren

I have been thinking a lot lately about the creation of patriarchy and how the hell we got here.

What I have realized is that every single transgression against women stems from this insane reversal of reality that destroyed the Paradise the Goddess created for us. As Monica Sjöö & Barbara Mor wrote:

> "A most unholy trinity dominates the patriarchal tradition: rape, genocide, and war. This trinity is an ideological machine, grinding out incessant warfare, power politics, exploitation of everything exploitable as some kind of objective historical process. And God the Father, in doctrine and in function, legitimizes all earthly patriarchs— bosses, slave owners, global corporations, male-controlled institutions and professions of church, state, university, law, medicine, military—which exist to capture and reify life process."[5]

We have been raped, beaten, verbally abused, molested, overworked, underpaid, enslaved... because of made up stories that fragmented powerful Goddesses and inverted reality.

The creation—and maintenance—of patriarchy is wholly responsible for the current state of the world. We cannot live with war, rape, and genocide anymore. We must stop the desecration of Mother Earth and of each other. There is no other way forward but to come back to the Mother.

---

[5] Sjöö, Monica and Mor, Barbara. *The Great Cosmic Mother: Rediscovering the Religion of the Earth.* HarperOne; 2nd edition, 1987).

Kali was the Primordial Mother. She IS the Primordial Mother. She cannot be contained within the confines of patriarchal thought or religion.

Tracy Pintchman wrote:

> "As the source of all that exists, the Goddess is the Mother of All. Even in those contexts where male deities are ascribed ultimacy, it is the Goddess who acts as the immediate source of creation, giving birth to the world from her own nature as divine creative power or as the material matrix from all arises. Such a vision of the female's role in creation reflects the biological realities of procreation, of course, for children emerge from the bodies of their mothers."[6]

Throughout the world, patriarchy has gradually been defragmenting the Great Goddess and replacing weaker versions of those Goddesses with their male gods. Sree Padma wrote:

> "In spite of these clear attempts to establish the superiority of the male deities over the independent goddess, in the actual religious arena, where the temples of Durga and Kali are concerned, the primary focus of the devotees is Durga and Kali, not Siva or Vishnu, who only function as nominal spouse figures."[7]

There is no place on Earth that has been made better by any patriarchal religion or splintering of earlier Goddess Religions.

I don't think most women have any idea how much their lives are annihilated by patriarchy. Unfortunately, we have a long way to go before we can even fully see our cages. The calming down of Kali's

---

[6] Pintchman, Tracy. "The Goddess as Fount of the Universe," *Seeking Mahadevi: Constructing the Identities of the Hindu Great Goddess.* Tracy Pintchman (Editor) SUNY Press; 2001.
[7] Padma, Sree. *Vicissitudes of the Goddess: Reconstructions of the Gramadevata in India's Religious Traditions.* Oxford University Press; 2013.

anger and imagery has everything to do with suppressing female power and rage.

I am tired of living in a world that was not designed for me or by me.

I do not accept that my daughter will be mistreated and abused in the same ways that I have been. I do not accept that entire populations of people can be massacred for land, profit, or religion. I will never forget the tens of thousands of children that have been killed these last months alone. I am furious that millions of kids around the world are hungry when we are spending billions of dollars on bombs and mass destruction.

Women should be fucking angry. Many of us are so beaten down we barely have a pulse. I've been there. Life in capitalist patriarchy does that to you.

Black Liturgist Cole Arthur Riley recently wrote, "Rage isn't the curse, apathy is."[8]

It is time to get angry. It's time to get livid. It's time to burn shit to the ground.

As Soraya Chemaly wrote:

> "Anger is an assertion of rights and worth. It is communication, equality, and knowledge. It is intimacy, acceptance, fearlessness, embodiment, revolt, and reconciliation. Anger is memory and rage. It is rational thought and irrational pain. Anger is freedom, independence, expansiveness, and entitlement. It is justice, passion, clarity, and motivation. Anger is instrumental, thoughtful, complicated, and resolved. In anger, whether you like it or not, there is truth.

---

[8] Riley, Cole Arthur. *Black Liturgies*. Facebook post November 11, 2023.

Anger is the demand of accountability, It is evaluation, judgment, and refutation. It is reflective, visionary, and participatory. It's a speech act, a social statement, an intention, and a purpose. It's a risk and a threat. A confirmation and a wish. It is both powerlessness and power, palliative and a provocation. In anger, you will find both ferocity and comfort, vulnerability and hurt. Anger is the expression of hope.

How much anger is too much? Certainly not the anger that, for many of us, is a remembering of a self we learned to hide and quiet. It is willful and disobedient. It is survival, liberation, creativity, urgency, and vibrancy. It is a statement of need. An insistence of acknowledgment. Anger is a boundary. Anger is boundless. An opportunity for contemplation and self-awareness. It is commitment. Empathy. Self-love. Social responsibility. If it is poison, it is also the antidote. The anger we have as women is an act of radical imagination. Angry women burn brighter than the sun."[9]

It is time we, collectively, burn brighter than the sun.

Let us now recognize, and honor, our Holy, Sacred Rage.

---

[9] Chemaly, Soraya. *Rage Becomes Her: The Power of Women's Anger*. Atria; 2019.

Kali I
Michelle Moirai

She Unlocks the Door

Francesca Gentille

When your anger
Comes out
It's going to wash over the world
Cleansing it
Purifying it
Changing it

It's going to sweep across the world
In flaming beauty
And leave the weak
Breathless
The stupid
Blind
And the stuck
Free

It's going to re-create
The pain of centuries
Into the power
Of wholeness
And the crime of truth
Into the strength of knowledge

When your anger
Breaks free
It's going to fly forth
In widening circles
Of meaning

Building up
The tower of babble
Until it reaches god
And then some

And when your anger
Has the ear of god
By his throat
It´s going to shake him
Over and over
Until he splits
In two
The God and the Goddess

And laughs
For a change
And cries for all the pain
And screams for all the anger
And becomes willing to start over

With your anger in charge
Of protecting children
And comforting the old
And nurturing mothers
And building families
And communicating across cultures
And renewing the planet
And tearing down slavery

Yes, your anger
Will masticate
Swallow and transform
The slavery
To power-money
pleasure-youth
Control and ownership

Into wind
And seasons
And water
And gardens

Listen
Listen closely

I can hear
Your anger
Calling
Calling out
Your name
Calling out your name
Loud and long
And it is coming closer

It is knocking
At your door
The one
You locked
And forgot
And walked away from
Years and years and years gone by

I can hear
Your anger calling to you
High and sweet
The clarion call
Of the words you have longed
And feared to hear

The call
Of the ending
And beginning
And dreaming
Of the world
As you know it

If you will just
Unlock
The door

Burn It All Clean

Claire Dorey

Accept the blood bowl Kali offers as a gift of knowledge so we can heal the deep soul wounding in all our wombs.

Recoil. Horror. Distaste. Revulsion. The first time I met Kali, I rejected her completely. I rejected her in exactly the same way I rejected myself. She reflected back at me what I saw in the mirror, a horror show. I couldn't look at her. I didn't understand her therefore I could not accept her.

There is a Kali in all our wombs. Blood. Tongue. A frenzy of arms. The road to accepting Kali is a long one. How can I, placid sponge and postmodern woman of minimalist times, understand this wild-eyed, torus-limbed, flame-throwing ravening, a whirlwind of destruction, incinerating and beheading humanity in a gratuitous blood frenzy? If I dare to look in Her eye, will I see a black hole of insanity reflecting right back at me? Why am I afraid of her promise of freedom? Why do I want to be contained?

The point about the Goddess is She is an evolving, creative, and unstoppable force that cannot be contained. Kali's iconography is complex yet I'm fixated on the meaning of the blood bowl and what I see as the Kali, Womb, Rage Trinity. What secrets simmer deep within the veins of this Goddess and can these secrets liberate us from the psychological trauma western patriarchy has inflicted on the uterus, our source of 'I'?

"Oh dear! There I am, Little Ol' irrational Me, my unruly womb doing what wombs do – misbehaving, wandering all over the place, getting all hysterical and leaping out of the window!"

Women hating know-it-alls told us that 'shouting therapy' – cussing a stray uterus – would lure it back into the body! Argh! Somewhere along the way we became victims to the lunacy the patriarch invented about our bodies. In recent history decisions about women's health have been made by men. Aretaeus informed us the 'wandering womb' was an 'animal within an animal' and Soranus said the 'wandering womb' could lead to 'hysterical suffocation' and death. The Victorians claimed menstruation was a disease. In the face of this self-perpetuating nonsense the patriarch had the gall to tell us we were hysterical, insignificant, and clueless.

Claggy. Sticky. Messy. Unclean. Source of shame. Source of poverty, frustration and stopping us doing things. Battle ground for human rights. It's the bit they cut out when it goes wrong because it will go wrong, because women are wrong, therefore wombs are wrong. Body rhythms and natural cycles were and still are 'women's problems'. Better not talk about them. No wonder we hide what is 'natural' deep in the shadows.

According to various ancient, grandiose and obsessive philosophers, psychiatrists and physicians women have always been the wrong sort of human!

"The female is [ ] a mutilated male...." – Aristotle.

Charming!

Just like Kali's overflowing blood bowl, our wombs overflow with disappointment, frustration, and resentment. We should be celebrating our blessedly, beautiful, cosmically aligned self-cleansing system – tidal batteries, absorbing, processing, and storing emotion, then 'letting go' when the moon tells us to – tension floating away on the outgoing tide. It's a system that works very well when the planet we inhabit is in balance but when the female half of the population are battered by constant misogyny and the psychological dysfunction that is patriarchy our internal mechanics go haywire. Even the ocean cannot absorb all the toxins patriarchy throws into it, so how can our wombs be expected to do so?

This is why we need a blade wielding Kali to slice through patriarchal illusion. Shiva and Shakti – male and female energy – need to balance, yet the carnage in Kali's iconography implies this balancing act involves a brutal battle with ego!

Garland of skulls. Skirt of severed arms. Feverish eyes. Blood bowl offered at the end of an outstretched arm. The road to accepting Kali is a long one. It's the dark night of the soul, a journey into the black blood. Her knife hints at cutting deep to soul wounding at a cellular level where we must perform an autopsy on our first-blood; on every clot and debilitating cramp; every delirious night and bout of nausea; every miscarriage; every insult our lovers threw at us. To accept Kali is to revisit the cruel words of the father – the judgement, humiliation, and betrayal. It's revisiting the trauma of sexual violence, from catcall to rape. It's recognising the grinding effects of rape anxiety and navigating public space as a war zone. It's understanding how men project hatred onto 'the mother' and how this hatred has become a cult. It's understanding how fear has momentum. Men attack others. Women attack themselves.

All blood is menstrual blood. By offering the blood bowl Kali offers us the dark truth of our own consciousness. She tears down the 'cage of numb' the womb built around itself and begs us to stop yelling into the void and weeping on the inside. She tells us to replay every eruption of premenstrual howling and see why it was justified. No apologies needed!

To love Kali is to weep for ourselves and acknowledge the poison they poured onto our petals. Muscular tongue licking deep wounding open, exposing what is raw, so it can rise to the surface, turning the inside out, releasing the fire and the hurt, demanding we unbolt the pressure valve and let the dam burst, a bloody explosion of Red Rage seething and glistening with the threat of revenge. Frenzied, euphoric, orgiastic, intoxicated liberation – a life-blood revolution!

No one is more powerful than Kali's cycles. Nothing on Earth can stop her. Kali is sometimes black, sometimes blue, and always red. Black is chaos. Blue is the endless summer sky. Red is the blood cauldron. Self-fertilising darkness and calm before the storm; brooding void and temperate afternoon; balance and blockage; winter and spring; flow and pause; cause and effect; rage and serenity; youth and age; puberty and menopause, unstoppable cycles, and Time itself move right through Her. Kali is life and death and spontaneous birth. Blood of life. Blood of death. Incubator of ideas. Incubator of life. Destroyer of ego. Red Rage squirting from every orifice.

From Red Rage life grows and when the moon rises and tantra inhabits the deadliest shades of night, we can set down our offerings of Red Hibiscus between the legs of the Dark Goddess – wild red petals rippling in the twilight, unfurled pistil, a carbon-copy of Kali Maa's tongue.

"I meditate upon the divine presence of the Great Maa Kaali, the source of all primal energy, to bestow upon me peace and liberation." – Kali mantra.

Be still my beating womb and meet your Dark Mother. Open your body-mind to possibility.

"The Infinite Mind of THE ALL is the womb of Universes."
- Three Initiates, Kybalion: A Study of the Hermetic Philosophy of Ancient Egypt and Greece.

The seething vacuum of the eternal consciousness is the Dark Mother. Every woman houses this power deep inside her. Is this why western patriarchy invents lies about the 'unhoused' womb and why they weaponise menstrual blood and use it against us, treating our source of power as a sign of weakness? Is this why they fear the Dark Mother's recall and why they feverishly search for evidence the holy grail is an actual cup and not the womb of their own mother?

Where is anger? Where is the anger of the stripped back, postmodern woman of these minimalist times? Until recently I didn't even know that being female AND being angry was an option. Woman and anger, vagina and voice – not concepts the patriarch wants us to get to grips with. We get so used to self-censoring, lowering our voices, and listening to our own silence we forget Holy Rage is part of our inheritance – a gift from our Dark Mother.

Walking the therapeutic path to self-acceptance I searched out anger in a litany of clots and cramps, eventually finding it at the end of a long list of emotions relating to suppression: fear, resentment, disappointment, frustration, jealousy, judgement, self-loathing, mistrust, criticism, anxiety, unworthiness, shame, depression, trauma, regret…

I found the word 'anger' but still couldn't feel the emotion. That came later, great torrents of it, when I learnt what the patriarch had done to women: the torture, the silencing, the inbuilt systematic violence, the erasing from history, the genocide. Then I became Kali. Trapped scream barrelling out of me like a flaming flash flood, burning away the filth they tarred me with. Primal, savage, raw, brutal, passionate, bloody beautiful Rage, a bubbling cauldron of wrath unleashed, but also a fine wine, fermented over lifetimes, with subtle layering underpinning the flavour – resolve, determination, compassion, self-love, and the desire to seek out wise soul sisters and work toward change. Holy Mother Earth! Holy Kali Maa! This is Holy Rage!

In the hands of the novice anger is a blunt tool but riding the Rage wave is to ride a wave of certainty where Rage is considered a beautiful thing.

"Bitterness is like cancer. It eats upon the host. But anger is like fire. It burns it all clean." -Maya Angelou

Talking to the cosmos is a forgotten art. Women whispered with the moon and tides in the language of flow – the language of tantra and sensory experience. Kali Maa is Mother of Time and all women were Time. From ovum to Goddess women were the calendar. Women were the juice of the cherry and the forest fire and we felt our way through the seasons with dirty fingernails. But patriarchy weaponised silence and shame and used them to disconnect us from the vast moon cycles moving through us, our source of power.

Without balance, masculine energy is unreasonable and chaotic, constantly taking humanity to the edge of destruction, using violence and threats of annihilation to maintain equilibrium. Being female is equilibrium. We are cyclical beings, four mini cycles per month, thirteen a year, continually evolving and balancing. Kali's eternal dance is a gyroscope, spinning and aligning with cosmic forces, seeking balance and within Her armageddon there is energetic creation not senseless MAD, mutually assured destruction.

Sisters, let's harness our Red Rage and reclaim our blood rights and human rights, as visionary, ritualistic beings – birthing lives and birthing free flowing thoughts and ideas. Paint the town in shades of rebellion: scarlet, ruby, carmine, vermillion, cinnabar, crimson, hot chilli pepper red and Hibiscus. With cherry lips and gyrating hips we will flood the streets with sensory experience and an unstoppable tide of female wisdom. Kali is rising. Female energy is rising. Let's return to equilibrium. The future is female and Kali says it will be bloody beautiful.

The Kali Principle

Jaclyn Cherie

I was one of those "too much" Women.
Which is crazy to think about because I struggled for a long time to take up space, until one day I realized I take up space in this world without trying.
And, so many of my Sisters do too, and they don't even realize it. They are all too much Women, as well.
They, like myself, have been told to water themselves down, be less opinionated, be less emotional; don't be too loud, don't be too independent, don't enjoy sex too much.
Don't be too much.
Too much. Too much. Too much.
It echoes in our heads and hearts.
So, we shrink ourselves.
Our bodies.
Our voices.
Our thoughts.
Our dreams.
We don't want to be the girl who is too much.
That's where Kali comes in.
She is the embodiment of the too much Woman.
She is destruction embodied (think of Her as the Tower Card).
She is time.
She is death.
She is justified rage.
She is the void known as the Cosmic Womb.

Kali Mask

Lauren Raine

From The Masks of the Goddess Project – used in performance.
masksofthegoddess.com

KALI

Lauren Raine

Once upon a time,
The world became populated by demons.
They filled the world with their insatiable greed
and reproduced themselves endlessly

>They ate the light of day,
>They soiled the air
>They consumed the trees,
>They swallowed the waters
>They devoured the lands

Eating, eating eating! Fill me! Fill me!

Until there were no more things of beauty made
or new dreams dreamed
or children born.

The Gods called to Me
The unborn ones called to Me.
The ravaged world called to Me.

The time had come to say Enough.
And.....NO MORE!

***I, I am
the Goddess of No More!***

I, I am
  the one who devours
I, I am
  the shadow,
  the flame,
  the dancing feet

I, I am
 the Mother
 of all those
 who are yet to come!

Jai Ma, Kali Ma!

Lauren Raine (1999)

Voice of Kali

Jonita D'souza

I have experienced several Kali moments since the beginning of my life but never knew how to name them. I used to call them my 'f#$k it' moments.

I was born in India and Kali has been a well-known figure ever since I remember. She was portrayed as the angry tantric Goddess, to be frightened of. People generally invoked her mantras to call in any kind of destructive force. I witnessed several instances when a woman got angry and ridiculed as – 'there she goes... she is having a Kali moment!'

Being an empath and introvert, I found really hard to connect with Kali in my younger years.

It is only when in my late 20s as I embarked on my journey of embracing the various facets of the sacred feminine, I officially met the Kali moment in all glory! I was brought to my knees several times as I navigated through my emotional shadows. I spend hours crying on the floor in the pool of my own tears not understanding where and how had I been holding such dense emotions for this long. I felt a lot of anger bubbling up. At first, I felt angry at everyone around me and then I felt even more angry at myself for all the moments where I did not stand in my truth. In that moment of total helplessness, Kali Ma appeared wrapping me with a warm loving blanket. It was a visceral feeling of finally understanding the fierce loving grace of Kali Ma. Lovingly she said it is normal for women to feel the anger, rage, pain, its revelation, its liberation. These words somehow comforted me.

She made me realise the pattern that had been keeping me disempowered – the pattern of self-sacrifice! It was no longer about society, my upbringing, government, patriarchy – but me!

Ever since she frequently shows up in my life each time, I fall into the unconscious pattern of self-sacrificing my life-force energy to make everyone else around me comfortable.

One recent moment was a fine day filled with a busy schedule in a noisy environment. There was an ongoing refurbishment work at home. I was sifting through my daily household chores, whilst working on an ongoing business launch and making sure my loved ones are taken care of for the day. As usual, I started my day with my morning prayer invoking support to get me through the busy day but got carried into the chaos.

Soon the electric power went off due to some short circuit, my food was burnt, my husband cramped his foot, my sales website ran into some technical glitch, my grandmother called in asking for support, I got my period earlier than usual and I lost my cool.

I shouted at everyone, ran into my bedroom, locked the door and started rolling on the floor crying and screaming. I felt betrayed by the universal forces. In this moment Kali Ma touched me once again.

As I was laying in the pool of my salty tears, she held me to remind me that my worth is not in all the 'doings' of the day and that I need to let go of this belief.

I said – 'I don't know how!' She said – 'Become fierce about doing 'nothing' for a certain amount of time each day and sit in that discomfort.' I did exactly that.

For the next 3 days, I allocated a good half hour of simply sitting in silence, watching life go about around me, things falling apart and doing nothing! It was difficult, I felt selfish, and I was very tempted to give-in, but I trusted Kali's guidance and sat in the discomfort. I prayed to Kali to intervene. My body was intuitively guided to hold the Kali mudra. On the 3rd day, I noticed that me stepping back from the 'doing' created room for life to provide for me in ways that I had not imagined. This was a profound realisation.

As they say Kali can only destroy what is destructible. I experienced un-necessary chores – that I had taken the over-responsibility for – either no longer valid or being taken care of in some other way.

Ever since, especially on a busy schedule, I allocate 5 minutes of holding the Kali mudra and just breathe. I include this in my morning practice, and I let spirit meet me halfway. I allow universe to be the co-creator in my life rather than being in the illusion of doing and getting all things done by myself and beautiful synchronicities occur.

Kali showed me how sitting in my discomfort and being a witness, without falling into the conditional behaviour of 'doing' can be revelatory to my own awakening and guide me to take inspired action rather than the busy-doing!

Often Kali moments are projected as big events in life and that's true for many of us. However, Kali also reminds us that our ultimate power as women lies in destructing the layers of ingrained patriarchal conditionings that are keeping us in a numb-busy-cycle. The name Kali comes from the Sanskrit root word 'Kal' which means time. We can call upon her to create time that truly serves us!

Kali's two right hands are shown in abhaya mudra (fearlessness), and varada mudra (blessings).

Holding this mudra allows me to tap into my power of witnessing time, this in turn opens doorways for receiving wisdom. Try it out for yourself.

Ever since my encounter with Kali, I have been able to channel deep loving wisdom of the dark feminine in contrast to the scary portrayal of power. Kali Ma liberates! May she liberate you.

Living and Loving Holy Rage: My Personal Journey

Dr Lynne Sedgmore

For me, understanding holy rage in our own lives is an important part of knowing and accepting the fullness of who we are. I share my journey with holy rage as an offering to support you in your own journey. The two words offer an important paradox, especially when presented pictorially, as Kali, in female form. Placed together they challenge the conventional patriarchal view that rage is unacceptable in women. They also transform rage into something sacred, positive, and beautiful.

I have lived with a conscious sense of rage and anger all my life. I feel like I was born angry, angry at the state of the world, angry at all the social injustice around me, angry within my family, and furious at patriarchal society. There was lots of anger, sometimes expressed through physical violence, in the working-class community I lived in. While knowing that my council estate was by no means perfect, I was angry at the way in which those of us who lived there were dismissed and considered to be lesser than anyone else in the social and economic structure of society.

Most of all I remember being angry at the way I was treated as a girl and young woman. Outraged by the way women around me were treated as lesser than the men, given so many constraints, and denied many opportunities.

I became a feminist at a very early age, out of anger. My brother was born when I was fourteen, the first and only boy after three girls. I saw the sheer delight of my father and realised the special and extra significance it meant to be born a boy. I was genuinely loved by my father but in that moment, I saw the truth of patriarchy – how by just being born as a biological male you had preference and privilege. Deeply impacted by that moment, I consciously explored feminism. At seventeen I became a second wave feminist warrior of the 1970s in the UK.

These were my glory days – fighting patriarchal injustices, going to demonstrations, organising pickets of sexist comedians, placing stickers that said this degrades women on sexist literature and posters, setting up a range of consciousness-raising and fat as a feminist issue groups, organising reclaim the nights, joining picket lines of striking women, demonstrating for a woman's right to choose, supporting black women, and LGBTQIA+ liberation. I helped to set up a women's refuge, squatted in a local authority empty house which was turned into a rape crisis centre, and facilitated women's literature groups.

My heart soars remembering it all, my fabulous, exciting, hopeful, committed angry feminist glory days. I absolutely loved being a full-time feminist activist for ten years, genuinely believing that we could bring about a fairer more equal society for women, making the changes that would lead to a society that doesn't oppress anyone.

This warrior work was steeped in anger. At the time I called it "my transformational righteous anger". Today, thanks to Girl God, I much prefer the term holy rage.

Having described my rage and anger, how did I access the holy? When I was nineteen, I got pregnant, unintentionally, and chose to keep my baby. While I was doing all the feminist activity described above, I also became a mother three weeks into being twenty years old.

This was an extraordinary experience that did two things. Firstly, I began to see the world through the eyes of being a mother and all the ways in which mothers are not seen, are disregarded, and impeded. This increased and fuelled my anger even more. How could such an important role of bringing our children into the world be so devalued and disrespected?

I felt the daily frustration, irritation, and difficulties of the lack of support for new mothers struggling with so many changes in their lives. The struggle of getting onto a bus with a pram, the lack of facilities for children in cafés and public spaces, the taboo of breast feeding in public.

I was one of the fortunate new mothers who didn't suffer from postnatal depression. Having a baby at such a young age was really tough. I was at university so I didn't have to cope with a full-time job yet my whole world changed dramatically, both internally and externally. I had a devoted partner who shared the childcare with me, and a child who was easy to love and be with, and still it was exhausting and overwhelming at times.

Having a baby brought up all sorts of mother wounding about the relationship with my own mum, and any anger I felt towards her. The work of Bethany Webster[10] has been incredibly helpful to me in healing my mother wound. I recommend her work to anyone wanting to heal theirs. Fortunately for me my mother lived until eighty-six so we were able to share this work and heal both our anger issues together before her death.

This poem expresses the mother rage I experienced at one time in my life and was written on behalf of all mothers and daughters.

---

[10] Webster, B (2021) *Discovering the Inner Mother: A Guide to Healing the Mother Wound and Claiming Your Personal Power*, US: William Morrow.

Cooking
(daughter to mother)

What do I do with this raw rage
boiling and bridling to unleash?
Numbing of pain with folds of fat
and feasts of food.
Your cautious life is safely served,
shared on tiny plates,
meagre emotions portioned out
in deadly sifted deeds and words
to soothe and calm your pain.
My appetite unmet — erupts —
I pour out molten liturgy
of red hot larvic words
that wound and waste —
burning us both.
To no effect —
all you share is
petrifying frozen glare —
defences high —
protecting you.
No skill to calm your ever angry,
hungry child —
my constant rage
still waiting to be fed
with unconditional love.

Becoming a mother opened me up to the power and holiness of experiencing unconditional love. Alongside the rage and anger I felt as a new mother towards society, I also experienced the most amazing unconditional love for my new baby girl. This did something important, deep, and profound for me.

This poem is written about a moment when my child was a few days old.

Mother Love
(for baby Keri and all new mothers)

First sight of you absorbs me whole
dissolving into oceanic mother love.
My service to the world twice births —
through you and through the
fragrant flowering of my heart.
No magic potions here or fairy mother wand —
just me — alone — post-birth —
with open soul,
and you held tight in my trembling arms.
On sacred ground I name my promises deep and true —
Know you are loved and your true self,
Know always I am here,
Nothing I will not do for you...

I kept my rage at social injustice and the desire for a better world through my activism, but internally something in me had opened and softened and was very vulnerable. A feeling of sacredness also arose.

I began to explore the women writing about feminist spirituality and Goddess spirituality in the 1970s. I loved the work of Starhawk, Mary Daly, Carol P. Christ, and Judith Plaistow. Exploring Goddess spirituality was another extraordinary life changing experience for me.

I genuinely believe that reimagining the divine as female is a radical disruptive feminist act and is empowering. I did then, and I still do today. For anyone interested in feminism and Goddess spirituality I write about them in my book and teachings of the *Goddess Luminary Leadership Wheel*.[11]

I remember the first time I met an image of Goddess Kali. Wow, here before me was my angry self – depicted so powerfully, the fierceness, the visceral rage, the desire to destroy patriarchy, the cutting through of the sword, the skulls, the blood – and so much more I couldn't even articulate but felt true. This encounter absolutely transformed me. I was aware of the righteous anger of Christianity, but I had never really experienced directly in such a raw visceral way that anger and rage could be considered divine. Kali was rage personified, yet she was also an image and depiction of the divine, She was sacred and holy.

This was a profound liberating and healing experience for me. I explored Kali and went to India to experience her more directly from within the Hindu tradition.

Thanks to Goddess spirituality I began to accept the ongoing rage and anger in me as part of who I truly am in my fullness and my divinity and my wholeness. I began to ask three questions: *How do I stop being run by anger? How do I stop my internal suffering? And, how can I use my anger more skillfully for myself and others?*

Amidst my activism and life as a mother I was feeling suffering in relation to my anger. For most people anger is unacceptable, especially in a woman. At its worst my anger led me to some destructive acts that harmed or frightened other people. I received lots of comments on how scary or intimidating I was. At times my anger felt nasty, uncontrollable, disgusting and

---

[11] Goddess Luminary Wheel Website:
https://goddesstempleteachings.co.uk/goddessluminary/
Lynne's Personal Website:
https://www.lynnesedgmore.co.uk/

undesirable. It was running me in a way that depleted rather than energised me.

Over many years through therapy, woman's circles, spiritual formation, and Goddess spirituality I learnt to understand and befriend my anger. I went on workshops to release my wild woman. I drummed before fires and expressed my rage on the land. I learnt to consciously know my anger. Eventually I began to express anger more skillfully rather than being run by it. I could feel and recognise my anger without needing to act on it. I could also be as fierce as Kali, cutting through gaslighting, societal constrictions and the negative and unwanted projections of others. I also learnt that for many women their anger has been suppressed and they need to learn how to get in touch with it. My *Goddess Luminary Leadership Wheel* includes a path of power, fire ceremonies and ways of releasing and viscerally knowing our personal power, including anger.

A self-awareness process that has helped me tremendously with my anger is understanding and working with the Enneagram.[12] I identify with Enneagram type eight. Imagine my relief when I realised that my whole personality structure is fixated around rage and the Enneagram provides a clear process to work consciously with my anger. I discovered new levels of insight. Only when I accepted, without resistance, the power, potency, impact, positivity, and importance of my anger did my suffering begin to relax and fade.

I genuinely believe that by experiencing and accepting holy rage as part of our personality and our divinity we can integrate and harness our anger and rage more skillfully and gracefully. We can be both fierce and compassionate. Holy rage inspires us to action; it mobilises us to act on behalf of ourselves and others. It can be a

---

[12] Riso, Don Richard and Hudson, Russ (1999) The Wisdom of the Enneagram: The Complete Guide to Psychological and Spiritual Growth for the Nine Personality Types, US: Bantam Books.

genuine act of service to changing and improving the world. We can use our rage to liberate ourselves, our sisters and anyone who is oppressed. Holding both rage and holiness enables us to make choices on how we bring both into the world.

My whole life has been a journey of understanding, integrating, and expressing my easily accessible anger in its many forms. I have learnt to love my anger and to transform it into a valuable important spiritual expression of something holy, precious, and invaluable. I now advocate that holy rage plays an important role in society. I now live, love, respect, and revere holy rage. It has played an important part in my life and is needed for women within a patriarchal society.

I hope that sharing my journey can inspire and support you on your own unique journey of holy rage.

Blessed Be.

Invoke Kali

Sonee Singh

Destroy what is old and rusted
Clear the dust in the being
Soul, Mind, Spirit, Body

Banish and send it to oblivion
Suck out and cast away the gunk
Damp, Dark, Old, Meek

Burn my whole being
Letting in the new
Sparkly, Shiny, Squeaky, Clean

Harness the warrior spirit
Unleashing the light at the core
Power, Heart, Blood, Gut

Shine so bright it blinds
Dance fiercely conquering demons
Fear, Doubt, Hesitation, Uncertainty

Bring in transformation
Usher in love
Myself, Whole, United, One

*This poem was first published in Sonee's poetry book: *Embody.*

Kali of True Vision
Kat Shaw

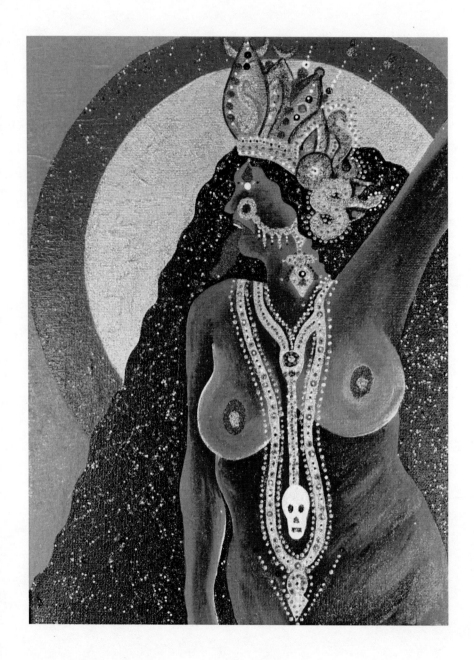

Kali's Gift of Holy Rage: The Lifeforce of Woman

Kay Louise Aldred

Holy Rage

The lifeforce of woman.
The volatile womb.

The volcanic force of Gaia.
The tsunami of aliveness.

The absolute NO.
The defender of the vulnerable.

Red. Hot. Destructive.
The fire that burns untruth to the ground.

The birthplace of Phoenix.

Goddess.
Unstoppable Feminine.

Kali's Gift

My relationship with Holy Rage is in its infancy – despite being 48 years old.

It has been a significant aspect of perimenopause and what I can say – without hesitation – is that it saved my life.

2016-17 were two full years of absolute RAGE. Not healthy anger. Pure rage. Which tore through every memory, thought, action, relationship, and life situation. I was completely ruthless, 'out of control' (at last), spewing volcanically, years of suppressed emotion.

As I sat down to write this, I tried to remember a time prior to 2016 when I had felt pure rage. My only recollection was in the late 1990s when my parents – combined with complex, mental and physical ill health needs – held me hostage in an all-consuming care role. This was whilst I was working full time teaching adolescents, trying to prepare to get married. I was also still in my early 20s and so not, in any way, shape or form, a mature adult myself.

I threw a glass across the kitchen. That was it. A tiny eruption followed by an immediate return to composure – internalisation, numbness and shut down.

I continued living, for another 20 plus years with no boundaries – constantly giving of myself and energy – expressing no personal needs to anyone.

Prior to that, the only other two times I can remember experiencing anger of any sort were in arguments with girls as a child.

Aged 8. I was a fireball. Defending myself against name calling, perhaps too zealously, swinging the name caller around by her ponytail. What I learned from the resulting disproportionate shaming and punishment at home was that when I was angry, I was an unbelievably bad girl!

Aged 15. After a year of habitual bullying, on one occasion I retaliated with a slap. Which then escalated into me being gang beaten and hospitalised. The learning from this expression of anger was that my life would be put in danger if I defended myself.

During perimenopause I have reflected on my rage and anger 'programming' and its origin.

The males in my family of origin lines were emotional. They were co-dependent, unstable, and actually gentle, although needy. They displayed no rage, let alone anger.

The women were a completely different story.

On the maternal line they were bitter, cancerous, festering balls of resentment. Gossiping, projecting, blaming. TOXIC. On the paternal line, repressed, religious, good girls – with no outward expressions of anger – only an overspill of internalised rage as self-destructive suicidal tendencies, attempts and unfortunately in my aunt's case, success.

I was trained to be 'good.' To be non-emotional, un-spirited and non-boundaried. To soothe and serve men emotionally and to be the dumping ground and a container for the women. I was conditioned to be (certainly for external appearances) saintly, calm – a Mother Mary and Quan Yin model. I was conditioned to save, and I was conditioned to serve, everyone but myself and offer my mind, intellect, resilience, love, energy and unfortunately my body.

When I had touched into rage at different points in my early life I was conditioned to be terrified of its qualities and power. So, I closed it down, fully. I repressed it, held it in and 'took' everything that was discarded onto and thrown at me.

I was abused a lot.

Without going into the details of complex trauma and ACE (adverse childhood experiences), needless to say a lifetime of abuse, lack of boundaries and self-representation took its toll physically. The gradual breaking down of my nervous system health which started with eczema, then menstrual and digestive issues, stress, mood instability, chronic migraine, chronic pain and reached its climax with fibromyalgia.

Eventually, following a serious accident I had a breakdown.

Which I can see now was the best thing that has ever happened to me. This was a breaking down of pretence, suppression and of denial of anger and emotion.

It was a BREAKTHROUGH and BREAKOUT. It was my doorway to liberation.

Holy rage, the gift and energy of Kali began to flow quickly as a broke out of the generational prison, which laid the foundations for the restoration of my boundaries, my body, and my health.

Kali gifted me back my life.

It is an ongoing journey. Kali's energetic 'current' and 'frequency' is the strongest feminine force I have ever experienced. It is akin to the ferocity of a body birthing. It is the power which manifests the Soul into flesh. It brought me into relationship with the holiness of my flesh and ALL my bless-ed emotions and mentored me in reclaiming NO as the word of the Divine.

Holy Rage has fuelled me to reveal my truth, out abusers, call out gaslighting and the stonewall aspect of psychological and emotional abuse. It had put me in a sphere of safety and supported me to reclaim my own space and boundaries. Once I felt Holy Rage in my veins, within my blood, the ongoing healing process of the plethora of physical illnesses I was diagnosed with began.

Holy rage is the cry of NO MORE and THIS STOPS NOW.

It is the backbone of my Shamanic Self – who journeys down ancestral lines and cuts the cords of dysfunction and soul retrieves liberty of future generations.

And once my personal redemption was well underway the Holy Rage of Kali opened my eyes to the collective captivity of woman and then of society as a whole.

Holy Rage is a gift Kali is offering us all now, especially us fledgling Elders (those transitioning through perimenopause, moving into Crone). It is the energy we need to advocate for justice, equality, and the protection of the vulnerable, and the birthing power of activists campaigning for shared power and harmony, the reclamation of embodiment and the dismantling of the patriarchy.

This is where I am currently. Fuelled by the elixir of my lifeforce – my sacred no – now tempered – my Holy Anger. Less rage, more anger. Calling out traumatic and patriarchal paradigms, relationships, and structures within institutions, like education and the church.

I see things clearly now and I am coming for it with my Holy Anger, flanked and fortified by the destructive Holy Rage of Kali – for which I am grateful.

Kali of the Undercurrent
Kat Shaw

Holy Rage and The Fullness of Time

Deborah A. Meyerriecks

There are times when I know I should be angry. Enraged. Yet, I feel overwhelmed, tired and the need to withdraw. It's hard to keep hope that anything will change for the better. The people in political and financial power who make decisions behind closed doors know what they are doing will cause harm to others, to the environment, and to society. They don't care. All they see is their profit margins growing as fast as their power. I should be seeing red. Enraged.

It's so hard not to feel overwhelmed, manipulated and at times, broken.

Often impossible to know the actual truth. I know that the harder information is shoved down at me, the harder it is to believe it.

While rage can often be blind, Holy Rage can be filled with clarity.

Holy by definition is to be dedicated or consecrated to god (or goddess) (or a religious purpose); sacred.

Sacrifice literally means to make sacred.

It is the giving up of something precious for a holy intention that makes a sacrifice a sacred act.

For myself, when I have in the past found myself in a state of rage, I understand that I left myself vulnerable. Sometimes, I think we must surrender the peace and calm security of anonymity we hold so dearly for the greater good to be served. There are times I find myself called to surrender myself, to be vulnerable for a time in order to receive strength.

Kali, (Sanskrit: "She Who Is Black" or "She Who Is Death") in Hinduism. While Kali and Parvati are not the same, Kali embodies shakti – feminine energy, creativity, and fertility – and is an incarnation of Parvati, wife of the great Hindu god Shiva. Kali is most often represented in art as a fearful fighting figure with a necklace of heads, skirt of arms, lolling tongue, and brandishing a knife dripping with blood.

My early memory of Kali is from a creation myth where Parvati, who is seen as a beautiful and well composed goddess, was created to help battle and subdue evil spirits. Paravati confidently marched into combat but when she was confronted by the demons, she furrowed her brow and her wrathful form, Kālī, emerged.

Kali is the feminine form of "time" or "the fullness of time." According to David Kinsley, Kali is first mentioned in Hindu tradition as a distinct goddess around 600 AD, and these texts "usually place her on the periphery of Hindu society or on the battlefield." She is a goddess who is considered to be the goddess of ultimate power, time, destruction, and change. She destroys to enable new creation.

 A reminder to how as women we are discouraged from this rage and battle. As daughters we are taught it is unladylike and unacceptable. We are expected to be beautiful, composed, graceful. Yet as Mothers. lovers. sister, and daughters we must remember how to engage this rage to survive. It is not a forgetting of ourselves. It is a remembering of who we are capable of becoming.

Kali is a reminder to not be lost to the blood-lust of the fight when provoked that far. The image of her tongue extended forth as she bites down on it and bleeds is from when she was deep in battle lust. Her husband Shiva appeared before her to calm her, assure her the battle no longer needed to be fought with such ferocity.

After noticing she trampled him, she stopped, biting her tongue in the moment of realization.

Because we have been denied the freedom to express our rage in times of need without the patriarchy resorting to derogatory slurs about us meant to discredit our thoughts and our reactions, too many of us have not had the guidance to learn how to use our righteous rage to evolve, grow, protect. We react without knowing how to direct our response for the benefit of why we needed to enter battle. In this blindness, we risk being blindsided and further victimized. To paraphrase the potent lyrics written by Wyndreth Berginsdottir (Karen Unrein Kahan) which we all have sung, we are our mother's savage daughters, or at least we have the capacity to be when we need and we must regain this skill-set in order to do more than merely survive. It is time to lead the charge and learn to thrive.

Rage or Holy Rage. In this time when we need to be reminded of the power we contain and are capable of wielding, we must invoke clarity with that power.

Often, there are those who would whip us into frenzy with limited information in the hopes we will provide the distraction they need while pointing us and our fury at those who are not in power to effect change but will see us as their foe when we attack.

Personally, I am willing to surrender my personal state of peace and tranquility, my insecurity about being enough to even effect change at all, to let that be my sacrifice. I do this freely in order to let my rage and fury rise and make it sacred. I invoke this process to receive Holy Rage with sharp clarity when necessary.

With the rise of Kali and righteous, Holy Rage, may we and our daughters embrace our right to not only be moved to anger but to respond with a rage of our own control. To be moved into action and not mired in place. For too long, quiet rage has taught us to hold our tongues. Being strong meant self-acknowledging how much we can absorb and withstand without reacting. How much we can take when we feel maligned or endangered or see others similarly afflicted.

No longer to ever be manipulated nor used as a pawn in another's cruel game. I have learned to accept, embrace, and invoke my personal sovereignty. To emulate and embody the energy of this dark goddess then direct her fierce power without fear where I see it is needed. These are some of the empowering lessons Kali will share.

I feel Kali Rising within me and I welcome this dark goddess and accept the gift of Holy Rage which may fill and empower me. No longer will I fear losing my well composed control or being silenced for I have made my fears and apprehensions sacred by willingly sacrificing them to Kali. I acknowledge the lesson of her bitten tongue and know I can choose how and when to raise and direct this potent energy.

Kali's terrible beauty includes its impermanence. She is the embodiment of self-sovereignty. The ability to choose to give up quiet, compose grace for fury and fire. The power that comes from knowing we decide when it's time to wield destruction of injustice and create change. Likewise, she is a lesson in regained composure, maintaining control, and resuming her gentle feminine state and embodiment of creativity and fertility in the fullness of time at the end of the battle.

Kali is the acceptance and full awareness that the end of a battle is most often not the end of the war. She is the reminder that we need comfort, rest, and love to be able to move forward. Kali both is the destroyer as well as the giver and receiver of love. She is never and always the same. She is complex, complicated, dangerous, nurturing, grace-filled and very much loved. She has by her own history, lost her awareness and herself to blood and battle lust. She has found her way back to who she wanted to be.

Either terrible or beautiful. Enraged or composed. Always her choice.

She teaches me that no matter what I am feeling or doing, it must be my choice. If it is my choice to avoid a battle and take time to rest and recover – or to take the time to quietly assess a volatile situation better or learn more of the pertinent facts of a situation before engaging in potentially heated discourse – it's all the right thing for me to do in my current cycle of the fullness of time. I am just reminded to refrain from becoming stagnant and that at another moment in time, I will be called to sacrifice my comfortable safety. I have long now sacrificed my compliance and I will no longer fear what may come from raising my voice, standing up, and being seen for who and what I choice to represent. Most especially, myself.

As Tom Petty sang, sometimes, there is no easy way out, but I will stand my ground and I won't back down. Not when my soul would cry if I did and especially not when such an act or failure to act would be a gross betrayal of self.

The fullness of time is always now. Kali is rising. Who will stand ready to learn her ancient lessons and wield her sacred powers of both creation and destruction as well as destruction for new creation?

Kali Screams

Sionainn McLean

Speak quietly. Be demure, be gentle, nurturing. A lady...

Kali screams NO.

Because we as women are abused, physically, mentally, sexually.
Our daughters stolen; our mothers beat. And we... our worth
determined if it fits the neat little bottles they have laid out:
Can she breed?
Is she pretty?
Is she humble?
Will she submit and obey?

Kali screams NO.

How fitting that this Goddess Kali Mata, the dark mother, this
goddess of ultimate power, time, destruction, and change shares
her story with Divine Rage. This Goddess who protects the
innocent by destroying evil, and She who bestows liberation.

Kali screams YES.

Fight. Roar. Do not hold back your rage, your inner power to
protect those you love, those in need, your body, your
sovereignty.

Dance, furious and with intention – you are no toy, to sit and obey,
demure and quiet. You, like She, seethe with sacred frenzy, letting
those who would harm you, who would oppress you and shackle
you know that you are dangerous, you are wild, and you are
untamable.

Kali screams YES.

Show your exasperation at these so-called rules for women.
Show your indignation that you are seen as less than a man.
Dance in the madness caused by their chains.
Let loose your passions.
Let loose your resentment, your temper, and your violence.
Fight with all the fury of a Goddess who will not be stopped until all who have done wrong have paid with blood and agony.

Scream with Kali, your voice erupting with righteousness with Hers.

This is my body; this is my place. This is my wrath; this is my fury. And only in balance, in justice, in equality will my bloodlust subside, only when the things that are wrong, are righted.

Scream with Kali. Scream with Kali. SCREAM WITH KALI.

Kali of the First Flame
Kat Shaw

Awakening

Ramona Chalmers

Goddess Kali is an archetypal force of power, strength, and emotion. As Goddess of life, death, and rebirth she uses her ability to destroy and dissolve old limiting paradigms and concepts, making way for deep inner transformation to bring us to a place of full expression and sovereignty.

My journey with Kali started a few years ago. As single Mom, I had experienced many events that shaped me; wearing mantles of loss, grief, and hardship that had left its imprints etched on my life. I had always been a strong alpha female, both as single parent and consummate professional, working hard and displaying a sense of fearlessness. I had done "the work" over the years, doing whatever it took to invest in my personal growth. I was constantly challenging myself to live out my best life, considering myself self-actualised, emotionally intelligent, and refusing to become a victim of circumstance. In reality, I was crippled with self-doubt, fear, and distrust of the world. Deeply embedded within my subconscious, was the need to prove that I had value while being burdened by shame, disillusionment, and hidden pain.

Although I was earning a good salary there was a deepening feeling of discontent coupled with a frantic longing within my spirit for something more. I did not know what I was longing for, but the feelings remained and strained towards the light, begging for acknowledgement. I was frustrated, as I did not understand what I was longing for and could not articulate this deepening sense of discontent. I tried to rationalize my feelings away, but the sense of disconnection grew wings. I was in limbo and going through the motions of my daily life. Beneath the veneer of the mundane, overwork, and always reaching for more was a deep truth waiting to be seen, acknowledged, and healed.

One day I simply screamed and raged against the Universe demanding the answers to my dilemma. "If anyone is listening, I demanded, I want to know:"

- Am I on track? If not, show me the way.
- What am I meant to be doing with my life?
- Is this all there is? Why do I feel so empty and hollow?

In a spectacular response to my rantings, it was no one other than the Goddess Kali who gleefully decided to take up the invitation to guide my journey and walk me home.

In short, a few weeks later the company I was employed by started experiencing serious financial difficulties, resulting in me not receiving a consistent income to be able to support my family's basic needs. As a single parent my highest value had always been being able to provide for my family. Over time the stress of trying to keep it all together resulted in a serious decline in my health, affecting even my ability to be mobile.

In short, I left the company even though I had nothing else to fall back on. The very next day I was interviewed for a job that paid far less. In order to honor my backlog of financial commitments I surrendered my rental space; moved back with family and sold off everything that I owned. In time the synergy and healthy energy in my new work environment had me gaining back my health, dignity, and ability to provide my family's needs, especially during COVID as I became the breadwinner.

Initially I felt that I had failed not only myself, but my family. Even worse, my previous employers started spreading derogatory comments about me, which fueled my anger and sense of betrayal. I felt defeated, afraid, and hopeless. It felt as if a gale force had entered my life and swept away everything that I had believed in resulting in me feeling very untethered and lost. I found myself stuck in the polarization of hope and hopelessness, anger and forgiveness, shadow and light; and power and powerlessness.

What remains in time of crisis, when life forces your hand, and you are stripped bare? We often talk about losing ourselves, or everything, but do we really? Like all journeys, some gifts only reveal themselves fully with the passing of time.

In a series of synchronistic events, I was asked to house-sit for a colleague, and during that time had a profound mystical experience that resulted in my first book of poetry called *Shadow Dancer*. After a particularly gruelling year which tested my health, emotional landscape, and personal belief where I was forced to make hard choices about letting go, I was ready to take my power back. I decided to work with a Life Coach and healer, someone I had never met and was based in a totally different country. During our first session she shared that her clan name as a healer was Shadow Dancer. Up to that point in my life I had been wallowing in my pain, victimhood, and story of persecution. I had an instant epiphany that helped me realize that life was guiding me and everything was happening for my highest good, not against me.

The divine speaks to us in a myriad of ways and during this experience it felt as if the heavens had opened up, gifting me with a sense of mysticism. I had a sense of a cosmic order being present in my life in a real and tangible way. We both had goosebumps!

More importantly, I realised that life's storms and detours are meant as a perfect and sometimes ambiguous redirection of one's life to bring us to our heart's contentment and aspiration. The storms in my life, and subsequent redirection of my place in the world from fallow ground to a place where I could bloom and thrive, now made perfect sense. As single parent I would not have left my initial employment and would have been stuck in having to continue to referee the power plays, shouting matches and pettiness that prevailed in my time there, fully believing as wounded healer that it was my burden to carry, and having to prostitute myself to stay in a space that was sucking away my life force and energy. This coach and healer became one of the many teachers that entered my life and journeyed with me as I moved towards soul-realization. I have learnt that everything is medicine.

In time, as I started paying attention to Kali's prompts and guidance, I found myself in a synchronistic dance that destroyed old habits, beliefs and patterns that had kept me stuck and no longer served me. It came with the realisation that Kali's goddess archetype appears like a thunderstorm shaking everything up in order to wake us from our sleep. In fact, what I had viewed as loss, failure and defeat was actually the start of a journey towards connecting to my power, strength, and deep authentic emotions to build a more connected life, and step into my sovereign power. No one was more surprised than I at my unexpected muse showing up and giving me the courage to be vulnerable in a way that opened my heart.

Together we walked through the pages of my life as I allowed the words to show up and reveal themselves through my poetry. I was emotional knowing that the time had come to write through, transcend and transmute remnants of dark matter in a way that honoured both the tribulation and the warrior.

I spent weeks crying for things I couldn't voice, the full realisation of a hero's journey, in fact, I cried for so many things that I lost count while I was writing. Most of all, my tears were for an incredibly brave young girl who had overcome insurmountable odds and yet bloomed in spite of it all. During this time, I struggled to fit back into a world which had forever shifted for me. I have been touched by many defining moments throughout my life, always knowing that something divinely miraculous was at work and I just had to lean in and trust that all would be well. I thus allowed the words and rhythm of each poem to reveal itself on the pages effortlessly. I subsequently wrote my life towards wholeheartedness – a homecoming of sorts. I was at the right place, at the right time for this pivotal moment of grace and wonder to reveal itself, and Kali stood at my side smiling.

Kali has helped me become more in touch with my inner landscape allowing me to cross the bridge onto a path from wounded healer to inner shaman. My initial resistance to my new path and fear of surrender was a stumbling block to understanding that beyond the veil there was only ever fierce love for me, and that I was slowly being guided towards freedom. In time my resistance and anger became a softening and leaning into, and I was able to walk this unknown path with more love, more understanding and more forgiveness than I had ever known was possible. As I journeyed further into the wild with her, I connected more to my divine inner feminine, a journey which continues to this day. My intuition was honed allowing me to connect with my raw, instinctual inner power and walk my new spiritual path with more grace and trust than I had ever known. I was now grounded in ways of being never experienced before and the voices and noises around me were silenced as I journeyed my unique path.

Letting go of limiting mental, emotional, and spiritual constructs as part of the journey became second nature as I continued on the spiral of evolution. I never was, and never would be, alone. Along with the deep inner work came the release and letting go of people, situations and places that were no longer aligned to my journey.; as well as owning and taking back my power in ways I had never done before. I found my voice, and it was here to stay! Kali showed me what was possible with a new sense of orientation, safety, and grounding. I know now that being firmly embedded to my creative nature will allow me to rebirth new possibilities in order to allow my wild, natural, and emotional energy to settle, express, and flow with ease through the river of my life as I pour out my medicine to the world.

My journey with Goddess Kali shows up in my poetry, which pays homage to those hidden personal battles we fight to overcome, when choice or circumstance chips away at our heart or soul leaving us hollow; struggling for breath. I know the power of words, either to uplift or destroy, as I have experienced both. Now I know that by the very act of expression, the time had come for me to honour a different strength, one birthed from fragility and vulnerability, and it was time for the walls I didn't even know I still had, to come tumbling down. Actually, if truth be told, it was more like a spectacular crash! How else would I pay attention to what was being birthed? Some stories can only be told with a heart cracked wide open.

All things pass, and we become the wiser and richer for it. As human beings we, in spite of the sometimes challenging and arduous circumstances we find ourselves in, possess an indestructible life force that can never be diminished. We have to learn to bloom where we are planted, whether it is in concrete pavements or in barren wasteland. What I have learnt is that the will to overcome, the desire to move towards love and our inner journey to find meaning in our suffering, becomes the raw material and emotive landscape of a true warrior. We are all significant, no challenge is insurmountable, and the world needs all its everyday warriors. No matter what the story of our lives is, we can dare to own and rewrite the ending of our own story.

Namaste!

Excerpts from *Shadow Dancer: Journey through Shadow, Psyche and Soul*

Ramona Chalmers

My initial poem to the goddess Kali was filled with rage, despair, anger, and grief. Being led to traverse a terrain filled with deep personal losses and learning to navigate the call of the soul while everything around me was fractured was the most difficult journey I had ever undertaken. I expressed my journey with her through dark terrain, into the underworld, in the darkness when not even the stars came out to play. I had to learn to rewild myself, leaving behind all that I had known, in order to release the shackles of patriarchy, poverty, powerlessness and lifetimes of generational and karmic stories that kept me tethered into playing small and hiding.

Demise
You dare to bring me here
Rake my flesh
Strip my bones
Intent on shriveling my soul
Yet you fail to understand
In combatting the beast
I have now become
A slayer of fiends
And your untimely demise.

As time passed, I was faced with the realisation that rebirth can only take place once destruction has cleared and paved the old. This meant being asked to be willing to let go of everything one holds true and clings to. Only through being willing to be naked and vulnerable in the midst of chaos, can we learn to traverse the deep inner landscape of the soul's journey towards sovereignty.

Awakening

Remove that cloak of shame and guilt, beloved,
The time has come to let it go.
Use this time to release it all,
You already are perfection personified.
Fill your inner chambers with love,
Wake up from your slumber, deep.
Know you now have infinite compassion,
Understand and forgive yourself–
Deeply
Fully
Lovingly.
This is how you leave the wasteland,
This is how you transcend indignity.
Understand that you are now adorned,
Nothing can ever diminish you.
In returning fully to love
You have come home to yourself.
This is what it means to be reborn–
Gentle, fragile, awakening.

Kali's presence in my life showed me that I was not helpless, powerless, or deficient in any way. She taught me to honor the journey behind me while recognizing that I was stronger than I realized, and in cosmic order everything was in divine order and timing.

Bloom

You might think that you are fragile
Yet push through concrete pavements
Thriving in opaque places
Under a cold sun
Blooming just where you are planted.

From barren wasteland, creating oasis
All this from hardened seed
Beautiful fragility
Blooming in no-man's land
Where angels fear to tread

My final poem to the Goddess pays homage to the journey undertaken and coming home. The Heroine's journey culminates in a deep, unshakable transformation and rebirth and soul realisation, where she learns to transform her pain into gold and pour her medicine out into the world.

Warrior

Harsh words and actions scarring innocent hearts
Uncaringly borne by tainted realities
Perception becomes secondary
As evil distorts our ability to revoke inhumanity

Subliminal messages we don't understand
Yet grow up believing it's the truth of a matter
When blackened hearts seek destruction over time
Its power destroys heart, soul and mind

Leaving scars unseen in deep recesses
Within psyche, and spirit, firmly cemented
Souls shriveled by harsh brutality and atrocity
When all should be nurtured, blossoming, cherished

Somehow I have come to understand
That the vicious sleight of evil hands,
Those who flay the deepest scars, are
Tainted, poisoned by their own iniquity

When my heart fully understands
I can choose light and not dark hatred
Malevolent power fades and diminishes
Whilst the phoenix and maverick in me ascends

With new awareness, consciousness, choices
My scars an opus of hard-won victories
Whose story is told of great battles wrought
In the silent chambers of a fragile heart

Annihilating darkness and gloom
Transmuting coldness, empty inner rooms
Into love and fearlessness, for all to see
This magnificent warrior that has become me.

Kali Ma

Sarah K. Grundy

Kali and her wild, bloody tongue projected onto New York City when she appeared in lights on the face of the Empire State building in art made by Android Jones and Obscura Digital in 2015. The Metropolitan Museum of Art showcases one of the most famous pieces of Kali art made by Ravi Varma, dating back to ca. 1910–20. Frequently featured in the New York Times—from the Manhattan apparition to our morning paper—Kali has officially pierced the heart and soul of our culture.

Kali is Shiva's Shakti (love power). She breathes fires of nourishing, loving devotion, and she liberates us when we need it the most. Mahakali crumbles shackles to ash and raises us in rebirth again and again. She embodies empowerment and reminds us of the extent of ours. When feeling powerless, defeated, vulnerable, wounded, defenseless and hesitant to act, we can return to Kali's story. Early myths tell us Kali's birth emerged in combat when grace would no longer suffice. She could inflict bodily harm with a mere thought, even to other gods, making them choke on their own blood just by looking at them.

Legend says Kali's tongue is red (and bloody) because she drank her enemy's blood in battle. This simple but powerful tongue-extending exercise is inspired by the vampire aspect of Kali's legacy and is a surprisingly powerful ritual. Do you know when a thought or emotion seems to bubble up not only in your heart, mind, and belly but also deep in your throat? If this emotion is something that no longer serves you, it needs to come out! Here's how to turn this rupture into rapture. When these feelings arise, this is not the time to swallow. This sensation signifies that it's time to subtly arch your neck back and stretch out your tongue as far as it can go (like Kali) to rebuke or expel this energy.

Kali is mother nature—the primordial, both supremely nurturing and devouring. When you call on Kali, do so with fire in your belly and intention. Be specific and call her by her name: Kali Ma, Divine Mother Kali, Mahakali.

Here is a mantra to evoke Kali's holy rage: I return to you the pain that you created and take back the love that I cultivated. For that is your burden to bear, and those are my wings to wear.

Kali of the Release
Kat Shaw

Speaking Truths of Holy Red Rage

Bobbye Middendorf

Red's alchemy now reclaimed
Bloodred of root beneath root beneath root
Rooted and so
Transmutes all embodiment into
Sea of Self-Love – grounded, swimming, immersed in self-love.

Eons hidden, lost, occluded, erased.
With fiery red self-love missing,
What is left but dust & fear?

& so Holy Red returns
In nick of time
Garb of Goddess & Kali's fierce visage
Her Fire-burning white-hot core
She is Red and
Holy and
Self-sovereign
Speaking all the lost syllables
From her HeartFire & SacredCenter
Holy Red
Holy Womb
Reclaiming wholeness as
Si-Star, Goddess, Priestess.
All Red
Renewed & revered.
Revitalized & redeemed
Rooted & resurrected.
The living Holy illusion-busting Mythos
Beyond known mythos
Preliterate Red speaks Truth
Breaking bounds of so-called propriety
Revealing mendacities beyond comprehension
She rises —

Holy.
Red.
Alchemical.
Rage.

Bobbye Middendorf, August 2022

An Introduction to Kali from My Future Self

Angie McCourt

Dear Angie,

I know things seem a bit out of alignment right now compared to what you've known, and you are not sure the direction you are supposed to take. This isn't new though as you've been through divorce and starting over in your personal life. The beautiful guidance in coming back to yourself was such an amazing experience during that time. See here's the thing, what is ahead will prove even more transformative and challenging yet fulfilling.

I want to bring to your awareness to Kali. She is a Goddess who is revered for tearing down old structures in our life and self – and guiding us through the journey to rebuild. Don't fear her although she does have a bit of a reputation particularly as the destroyer. She is here to help, and you'll come to Love her wholly in all ways she enters your life. You may not have recognized her in the past and that is why I'm introducing you to her now and sharing some insights into how she will play such an important role in your life over the next decades. You are meant for more. This is a big part of Kali's intention for change and transformation. Because you won't be the woman you are meant to be while on the path you are on right now. Although you rediscovered yourself, there is much to heal from, learn from, expand into and there are tests to complete. Finding true sovereignty is a journey.

You wanted this didn't you? As you journey over the next decade you will find points of misalignment between who you are, how you are showing up in your life, and your work. You will seek out complete transformation, change in life, a different way to be and live in the world. You will find in the pit of exhaustion that you are not enjoying the life you've built. There are aspects, but some areas are too overwhelming, and you'll want to change them. You will want a shift from old programming and expectations into

94

helping others. You won't even realize you are on this path for at least a couple of years but follow your heart and your intuition. When you feel pulled towards something new to explore and learn, go for it. When you become aware of a life lesson you need to learn, take it on fully. When you realize the misalignment in your work, make the change even if you fear losing safety and security. Trust me, you want this change and Kali will help guide you to a better way of being and living.

You might ask, who is Kali?

> "Kali is the creatrix of the Universe and she holds the power of time, rebirth, chaos, and destruction. She is a force to call upon to clear away what is no longer needed and to tap into a powerful energy of transformation. She is the Goddess to connect with when we are petitioning for complete change." -C. Ara Campbell, The Goddess Circle.

Her sword of knowledge has helped to destroy your ignorance. Her severed head helped liberate you from ego. She is the guide on your transformation journey.

Be open to transformation. As you've already found such great liberation in connecting back to your authentic self on your journey, you have witnessed transformation. You have felt the positive impact of rediscovering who you are. Kali isn't finished with your transformation. You have many life lessons to learn and ways of showing up and being to discover. What you have known your life to be with all the expectations will be a process of tearing down and rebuilding. This will allow your own personal transformation to occur. Embrace it, be open to it. You will find reconnection to others and nature to be the catalyst for your own continued transformation.

I ask you to trust Kali. Once you trust Kali you will see where she is trying to help you get to, who she is trying to help you become. You will come to love her deeply. As you sit at your altar and call out to Kali for guidance you will hear her love come through. She is here to help you break through what no longer serves your purpose or intentions. She is grace through a hurricane, she is love through fear, she is light through darkness. Don't waver on your trust or she will come more full force or back off and you will be in full chaos or in limbo. Accept and trust her fully.

The symbolism of Kali has visited you in 3 ways. Life and death. Creation and destruction. Nature and nothingness. These are the different aspects of how Kali can help answer our call for change and transformation. She will be there with you along the journey so remember to connect with her. Talk to her, share with her, cry with her. Ask her for guidance without fear of what will be unleashed. Be with her in love and don't shy from her no matter how hard life might become. Release your fear of the impact and results Kali could bring into your life and surrender to her.

Kali will help you transform. In nature and nothingness, she has helped you to reconnect to your body and realize how important this temple is to you. Aligning to the cycles of earth and moon you will feel like you flow more in life instead of resisting it. You need to feel the full numbness, exhaustion and overwhelm of your wounded masculine energy to realize how important your focus on your body is every day. After falling to complete exhaustion and overwhelm of doing you will release what you knew to be successful and allow for more. More love, more flow, more connection, more co-creation and moving out of isolation, force, and ego. The biggest lesson you will learn from Kali is to allow your feminine to come into balance. Of being instead of doing and to include others. Join and create circles and enjoy their wisdom, friendship, and love. To shift your role in your relationship with your new husband from one of control out of insecurity to that of receiving and affection. Allow Kali to guide you.

How much Kali will impact. In creation and destruction, Kali will help guide you through releasing what is no longer serving you. A job that is not fulfilling and will run its course. A fast-paced life that is not giving you space to just be instead of doing all the time. Her touch on your world will allow for the removal of what no longer supports your path. It will be time to let it go. It will be hard to let it go, but you will do it with grace and that is important to you. Although you won't realize the multi-year path Kali is laying out of setting up the creation even prior to the destruction you will see now how this was all a plan. Your awareness of the synchronicities happening around you and your ability to see things from a new light with an open mind will lay the path out for you. As you work through the destruction of letting go of the job, the home, and the life you had for decades you will make space for the creations. Kali will lead you through the spark of creating your business, writing your book(s), and launching your podcast. The commitment is yours though. You need to fully embrace your new path. Hard or easy as it may be. You will continue building on this path. Kali will be right beside you.

It will be hard. In life and death, Kali will bring challenges for your beautiful boys. She will test your unconditional love for them and will even take away from you your co-creation. One will have a major health challenge that will shift his direction in college. Be there for him fully and help support him with guidance and love. Then five years later your other beautiful son at age 25 with his future ahead of him will be the biggest test. While his life looks amazing and he has everything going for him, she will take him through him taking his own life. He is needed elsewhere and has fulfilled his contract here on earth. Kali will take care of him and ensure he finds peace. She will even offer miracle messages from him from beyond that will give you a sense of peace in your grief. She is not cold; she is the co-creatrix of this universe and he has an important role to fill. You will be devastated, but you will choose not to dwell in sorrow and grief and instead continue to be a light for him. Your days will feel like you are bouncing between dimensions and sometimes reality does not feel anchored, but this is Kali's way of giving you a view of the sovereignty you hold in this life. The power you use to create includes your own reality. It will take time, but you will learn how to use this power in love.

Kali isn't done. At the time I'm writing this letter you will be at a crossroads again in work and life trying to determine how to serve others while also being fully sovereign. You have healed from old work situations yet are still on the journey. This will be a big decision to go back into the world you escaped from while taking the lessons learned and putting in place protection of the life and way of being you have transformed into. This will be a big test, but you are up for it. You recognize how important it is to flow with life and continue to evolve. Kali will be there beside you throughout the journey. Be with her, listen to her and love her. She has your back and will be an important guide on your continued journey.

Reach out to Kali. All you must do is sit down, clear your mind, and call out to Kali. Invite her into your space. Connect to her using all your senses. Share what's on your mind. Release your ego and go deep into your heart for what you want to transform. Begin the next part of your journey co-creating together.

All my love on your journey.

Angie

Kali's Daughters (Sisters)

Molly Remer

We know the sound of howling
and the feel of fury,
of rage rising its head to strike
eyes cold and glittering.
We know how it feels
to stand under a storm-licked sky
arms raised and tears falling
hot and fast.
We know the sight of vultures
coasting on gray air,
wings wide and graceful
our own bones hollowing
as we remember
what it means to glide.
We know the winds
and how they whip and whisper,
the river and how it flows
and rumbles,
the easy tumble of water
parting gently over stones
and the ferocious cascade
that spills past its edges
and sweeps away everything
that stands in its way
without looking back.
We know hawk eyes
and eagle talons,
the silent swoop of silver owls
across the night.

We know how to walk
in the woods alone,
feet in step with desire
and senses alert
to both shadow and memory.
We know cauldron's fire
and yarrow's song,
the swift, sweet passage
of plum blossom
under the feet of bees.
We know patience and mystery
and the threads of magic
that stitch the world together.
We know the heart of the wild
and we feel its song
resound within our own chests,
fierce and fast,
sweet and strong.

Loving Kali's Dark Divine Rage

Tara Greene

I have been a vessel of Kali's fiery dark divine rage for truth since my first memories as a three-year-old. Her fierce rage coursed through me as wild temper tantrums against restrictions in my family and society. Through my teenage years and into my adult life Kali's energy guided and nurtured me. This energy, passion and strength evolved into deliberately defying authorities, medical experts, and falsehoods in the media and social structures and the machinations of Patriarchy.

I distinctly remember fiercely pounding my little fists and feet on the wood parquet floors screaming with anger at my mother and father who I knew could not teach me anything as they were asleep spiritually and were not fully conscious. I was frustrated from a spiritual higher knowing that I had come from remembering my past lives and being a multi-dimensional being and was frustrated to have to deal with these limitations. This was not just the three-year-old temper tantrums of "a spoiled child" as the many psychologists my mom took me to as a five-year-old later described me. It makes me wonder how many other labelled children and adults are simply more spiritually aware and are forcibly repressed with drugs and disempowered. I was labelled a wild child and my parents threatened to take me to the "Nut House" – the Mental Institution at 999 Queen Street of infamy – because I was angry. They put the fear of a patriarchal sky god who would punish me for daring to disobey and go against the confines of the "norm" and act out. This was in the very strait-laced 1950's.

Ever since I can remember, I was burning with rage as I saw hypocrisy everywhere – especially in religion. At eight years old I defaced a place of worship. I was angry at the unconscious, ignorant state of the world, raging at the violence, the mistreatment of women, the raping of mother nature, and knowing that it was the patriarchy – the demonic Colonizing, self-aggrandized "god given" force in all major world religions. I was unconscious as a teen that it was dark Scorpionic Kali of intensely blazing X-ray vision eyes who was using me as a vessel. As an angry defiant teen, I wanted to push that red button and annihilate the world in an atomic mushroom cloud to free it of its destructive energies to rebirth and regenerate itself in spiritual truth.

I raged at my mother as a child trying to wake her up out of her co-dependent doormat, passive aggressive shopaholic revenge as her only power in the world. My mother was terrified of my anger. She didn't know how to discipline me. I raged at my father for treating me like a girl for expecting me to just stand there and look beautiful and wait for some man to come along and take care of me. My mother admitted casually in her mid-seventies that she had been sexually abused by a cousin in her childhood home for years. She told her mother, who disbelieved her. In a flash I understood that I was acting out my mother's unexpressed rage from the cellular conscious memories of her sexual abuse – and frustration that her mother refused to believe her, defend her, and protect her.

Kali is a Hindu Goddess and historical records show she has been worshiped for over two thousand years. India has always worshipped the Gods and Goddess equally to this day even though Patriarchal culture has severely taken over.

The name Kali means KALA or force of time. Before the sun, the moon, planets, and the earth, there was only all-pervading dark space, which is Kali. She is both Death and Life bringer, Preserver of Nature, and the Great Mother in both her aspects. She is the feminine counterpart to Shiva. Kali is of the supreme unmanifested Brahman state. KALI, Black as the Void – she is the Great Womb of all, everything emerges from Her, she is beyond all space, time, and descriptions.

As Great Mother Night, She symbolizes the infinity of Time as Kala, the word calendar came from her name which means Time. She is timeless time. Without permanence she will continue to exist even when the universe ends. All qualities of good, bad, and dark do not apply to her. As we work with Kali we integrate and transcend duality.

Kali is All That Is. In Hebrew mysticism, *All That Is is* expressed as "Ain Soph Aur" which I intuit as the Limitless Light, Sophia's wisdom, which is all darkness. Kali is Death Bringing Crone/Hag Goddess so feared in modern western cultures. She is like Lilith, the original woman in the Old Testament. As life bringing Great Mother, she is Shakti, Shekinah, Isis, Mother Mary, Demeter, all birthing Goddesses.

Kali appears as two, four-armed or as the ten-armed Mahakali. Women are always multi-taskers. Often depicted as standing on Shiva's chest, a symbol of his devotion to her receiving her grace for destroying the ego.

Kali worship must have been transmitted to the West in medieval times by the wandering Romani gypsies, originally from India. In the Camargue, a region in Southern France near the Spanish border, west of Arles in Provence, a Black Madonna or Saint Sara-la-Kali is worshipped annually with a pilgrimage for a fictitious Saint Sarah at Saintes-Marie-de-la-Mer. Kali is thus connected to the story in the Davinci Code based on Templar hidden traditions of Sarah who was Jesus and Mary Magdalene's daughter too.

The western world fears Kali's destructive divine warrioress rage the most as it dissolves the ego, which can so easily be manipulated by sex in the media and controlled by corporations and governments and the belief in heroic allopathic Big Pharma. Kali loves cremation grounds and cemeteries and Tantric devotees. In Tibetan Buddhism she is like the Red Dakini, known as Dorje Palmo.

Kali was my fierce guide telling me to not listen to traditional western doctors when I got pregnant with my first child in 1978. Kali had me question the doctors about their Cesarean section and episiotomy rates, which outraged them. How dare I question their authority? She gave me the courage to trust my intuition in birth-giving Kali Ma.

Many years later my dear friend Edda West invited me to her monthly women's lunar pagan gatherings. She was interested in Sanskrit chanting and had been a follower of the great Yogi Muktananda. Edda had a beautiful singing voice and I loved to sing too, we would meet to sing and chant this KALI chant:

JAYA JAYA Kali Ma,
Jaya Durga Ma Ha, repeat 108 times.

This Sanskrit mantra was my conscious initiation welcoming KALI into my life.

Kali made me strong and fearless when my first marriage was destroyed by my ex-husband who suddenly left, taking our six-year-old son Elijah with him. I raged and raged. I cursed him as I had done in our previous past life.

I had major Déjà vu with a Tibetan Buddhist Lama in the 90's. He bestowed upon me a protective spirit guide called a Yidam. She is Dorge Palma/Dorge Phragma in Tibetan, known as a Tantric Red Dakini. A naked 16-year-old with a necklace of skulls, trident, a conch shell of menstrual blood, She destroys the ego and dances with desire for transcendence of Ego.

In Tibetan Buddhism she protects good from evil. When evil does not go away by virtue of love alone, Maha Kali rages up to scare evil forces from one's life.

Maha Kali, if worshipped with sincere and full devotion, will rid one of evil forces from your life. At this time of great negative oppressive forces in the world, almost everyone is afraid and has depression. We must call upon Kali.

As women's rights are eroded over Roe versus Wade in the U.S. and a Fascist like, feminist backlash reasserts itself in a world birthing into new dimensions of consciousness – Kali, like Durga would be called upon to right injustice of any kind.

Making a black altar to Kali and chanting Kali's mantra daily 108 times establishes a relationship with her.

I drew Kali in a series of paintings on paper years ago. This helped manifest her into bringing momentous change into my life. Since so many women are waking up to how we have been totally colonized in every way, Kali is the preeminent force to call upon to deal with the demonic transhuman agenda which has been unleashed full force.

We need to stop believing we must be nice. Stop the fear we will be labelled crazy or hysterical, which means wandering womb.[13]

We must be strong to manifest our souls as whole in the world. We must call upon KALI to let our rage BURN like a walking volcano or Pele, like a nuclear bomb, an uncontainable force of nature in service to transcendence.

All the emotional, sexual, spiritual, and mental abuses we have personally endured, plus all the abuses that our mother's experienced, and her mother experienced, and all the mother's from before recorded history; we were in their wombs, and we

---

[13] According to Wikipedia, "Wandering womb" was the belief that a displaced uterus was the cause of many medical pathologies in women. The belief is first attested in the medical texts of ancient Greece, but it persisted in European academic medicine and popular thought for centuries. The wandering womb as a concept was popularized by doctor Edward Jorden, who published *The Suffocation of the Mother* in 1603. *Suffocation of the Mother* was the first text on the subjects of the wandering womb and hysteria that was written in English." https://en.m.wikipedia.org/wiki/Wandering_womb

remember and we know, and feel it in our cellular memories, consciously or unconsciously. We know, and we are stronger because of it. This knowing runs in our veins and inhabits our flesh; we feel it in our bones. We remember this ancestral trauma of innocent women and children, herbalists, healers, midwives, and crones burned at the stake, raped, persecuted, shamed, and tortured. We remember consciously or unconsciously. Knowing in our hearts that this is why we have all reincarnated now, to enact Kali's righteous wrath. This is why we are made for this time, to bring karmic justice, to bring the world back into a loving, balanced Garden of Paradise within ourselves and all around us. Wrath brings us to a sacred marriage, an alchemy of the Divine Feminine and Divine Masculine, and all creatures in a loving balance, knowing that we are Infinite Beings, reading this text now.

We transmigrate different lifetimes as diverse cultures. It's time to get legitimately angry at all brainwashing which we have been told to ignore. Allow Kali to use that internalized rage as pure energy and to bring it into balance within. Kali's crazed Tantric followers were known as Thugee's, Spiritual Gangsters.

Kali is also the Great Mother protector coming from pure unconditional love. Allow Kali to come fully into your earthly vessel, into your womb and heart, so you can experience Her eternal truth and heal yourself,

The patriarchy and the cultural indoctrination. The New Age overly light denials of anger are designed to detach you from your power and your righteous anger.

Kali can help you to transform what is much of a living hell into a life of unlimited strength and compassion. Kali, as Mistress of Time, teaches us that the time is now.

Call on Kali to feel all your rage for transcendent Bliss – to right the wrongs and reinstate the memories of a world of love, peace, balance, respect, a physical and spiritual world based on the Divine Feminine.

A poem for Kali:

Kali, beautiful blackness of the void,
with your huge black tongue lolling out defiantly,
wild red eyes and disheveled hair,
Naked and skeletal, your black bones,
adorned with a necklace of bloody skulls
collected from demons as victory talismans.
She wears a skirt of severed human arms,
And carries a lunar crescent shaped sword, a giant sickle,
a trident, a severed head, and a skull cap to collect the blood.
She rages against all egoic enterprises and evil,
Accompanied by immortal serpents and a jackal of the dead.
Of timeless time, Kali, Infinite birth giving and death bringing Goddess.
Everything is created from your beautiful Darkness
and dies into the light.
I worship and entreat you to liberate my soul with unconditional mother love for infinity.

Sacred Fire

Tara Greene

Kali Speaks

Molly Remer

Untie the dangerous woman.
Unleash the powerful woman.
Uncurl the fierce woman.
Unbind the courageous woman.
Untether the wild woman.
Unloose the brave woman.
Unwind and unravel
the courageous and the curious
and explore,
wings unbound,
claws unsheathed,
hopes unfurled,
teeth bared,
and purpose unleashed.
Open the door,
fling up the windows,
slide off the shackles,
unburden the heart,
and fly.

From the Ashes of My Life
Wakanda Rose

Fire. The flames that bring you to your knees. Fire. When there's nothing left but your pain and that sudden spark that brings a warrior queen alive inside of you.

Nothing in life would ever be the same again.

It was 2019 when Kali entered my life with a powerful stomp, changing my entire life.

Everything I thought was me, every belonging, every part of my identity gone in a moment. A moment so fast it felt like the whole world slowed down yet was the quickest moment of my life. It was a car crash that changed my entire life. The careers I had built for years gone. The house I lived in gone. Most of my possessions having to go. Kali was only just beginning to bring her flames into my life.

Then... heartbreak over a man who could not love me in return.

I felt the full force of Kali in March 2020. A moment I remember fondly. A simple text from a man I cared so deeply about brought me to my knees. "I choose her not you". The pain I had been repressing perhaps for longer than I realised, suddenly tore out of me. The scream that came out of me, unearthly. The collapse to my knees, profound.

A choice became clear: *Do I become the pain and unleash it on the world? Or, do I sit in the flames of my own fire to become?*

I knew then I needed to descend into myself. I knew I needed to let go of my identity, the parts of me that had clung onto a man that fed sprinkles of breadcrumbs – and I had assigned my worth to him. Changing myself into what he was telling me he desired from me so I could keep him around. Believing he wanted children and love with me only to find him disappearing from my life a week later after saying this, having chosen someone else. The parts of myself that never chose me needed to be given to the flames. A man reflecting the deep neglect I had been given to myself.

The embedded societal programming so many women like me have of feeling we must change who we are to be chosen by others, especially some man. That a knight is going to rescue us and fall in love with us. No. I needed to be me despite what society may say. I needed to choose me even if it meant no Man would ever love me. I needed to be my own hero. And I did.

I never knew anger could be so delicious, so sacred.

Something rose within me. Boundaries. Fuck. This. I'm worth more.

Kali entering my life never felt like a sense of power over or being better than, no, it was me seeing I mattered too. My open heart to the world, and deep compassion to all was worthy of being gifted to myself too. A deep descending into my own heart to be felt by myself for myself.

Have I had thoughts of revenge, absolutely! Leaving my poop outside the workplace of the man who did not choose me crossed my mind. Thoughts of hurting, perhaps even killing the man who chose to race in a 30mph and later admitted in court to driving up to 90mph when he hit me and my dad, absolutely! And I allowed myself to feel it all. I would not gaslight myself, I would not abuse myself, I would not make myself wrong for any of these thoughts. No, a line had been crossed and I was in deep agonising pain. I sat in the fire of it all, welcoming this growth into anger, allowing myself to feel where my sacred no was and alchemised all this pain. For too long I had fawned and people pleased my way through life, I needed this Sacred Rage to reprogramme myself. So, I drank every bit of that sweet divine nectar.

I found Kali was not some "evil spirit" or "crazy being". No. She is an unconditional loving Mother. She sees our worth when we can't.

When we fall to our knees and have nothing more, she is there, waiting, holding, nurturing. Everything that was taken from me had to go. It needed to be destroyed in the flames. All the things I had clung to trying to keep some normality, sense of self and worth in my life, yet these things were all holding me back from who I truly was. Kali rebirthed me from the ashes of my life.

I rebirthed me.

October till December 2021, another dance with Death and feeling the profoundness of Kali yet again. Feeling inside all the traumas and heartbreak I had been through for my 26 years of life at the time. Yet, this near-death experience felt different, deeper, my relationship with my shadows more nourishing and loving.

Kali has shown me just how important the body is as part of this process, that yes, the mind and emotions deserve nourishment, as does the body. Our sacred divine human vessel. The key to the doorway of bringing the Divine on Earth that we are all seeking, yet forget it is within us, perhaps the most secret and scariest of places to venture.

Right now. 2022. I am rebirthing. Bringing all parts of me home inside my sacred body. As I write this, I have now faced my 3rd close to death experience. I've allowed that deep reality of death touch me so I may be inspired to live.

I've taken back my Crown. I've built the best relationships with friends and family that I can. I've gifted myself with an inner world that feels rich, yummy and has space for ALL of me, not just the parts society deems desirable.

I'm still deep in this beautiful human experience, feeling everything, dancing with life. Yet I know I'll always rise.

To end the suspense, no I did not leave my poop on a previous lover's doorstep and no I did not kill the driver who crashed into me and my dad. Perhaps that would have been the easier path to follow. This deep immersion into myself and the Goddess Path brought something else with it, something that is hard to put into human words. Yet it's something I feel deep within and know to be true. Allowing myself to re-emerge as the Fire Goddess – Kali, Freyja by my side dancing together deep inside.

Kali and I built my Queendom – from the ashes of my life.

A Message for the Unbound Woman

Molly Remer

She knows fatigue and fury,
grimness and delight,
hope and harmony.
She has been heart-centered
and heartsore,
serene and scattered,
centered and wild-eyed.
She has been slick with sadness,
drenched with delight,
alive with awe,
frozen with fear,
and crumpled with confusion.
She has been raw and worn,
rich with satisfaction,
dappled with doubt,
and ripe with certainty.
She has been shaken in her skin,
stripped to her bones
and restored to the sacredness
at the center of things.
She has known tender renewal,
savage beauty,
wild mercy,
and relentless grace.
She is the one who has walked
full-bellied
into wholeness
who unleashes her magic,
untethers her madness,
roars her truth
and sings her story
under both thunder and sun.

You've Got Hell in You

Sharyn Ginyard

Those words were told to me at a crucial age of adolescence by my father. When he first said them to me, I was crushed at the time and would have done anything to have not had him see me in that way. I had disappointed the only parent who I felt at that time loved me.

I believed him and felt so ashamed as I worked doubly hard to erase the black smear I had created.

I burrowed even deeper into myself to bury the traces of the bad self. Concentrating on being a good girl. The quiet, soft, obedient, kind, and polite good girl I told myself he was so proud of. As I hid behind a mask of hurt for not being allowed to be seen. I would smile whenever I received the minimal approvals that were rarely given like they were valued treasures. I would light up like a Christmas tree and want to do even more to please him. I even told myself at one point that my mom was jealous whenever she would scold me for not thinking for myself.

So, those were the golden days of illusionary fairy tales, tea parties in pretty dresses and blah, blah, blah. With an eye towards growing up and becoming just as unhappy as my mother.

I was born into the perfect setup of entrapment and enslavement to a system that manipulated me into believing that being the only girl in a family of four brothers made me somehow special. My brothers were presented as my knights. Sworn to protect their sister. But they were never around when I needed protection. In fact, I protected myself without realizing it better than they ever could.

You see, fortunately for me, Kali was a shadow part of me, an inner strength that never really left.

115

In my younger years Kali was that part of me that showed up every now and again at the unfairness of it all when she wanted something that she was being denied solely based on being a girl. Four brothers against one girl in the era of the 1950s and 60's, became what for me was to become the manipulative good girl's tool bag of my feminine capacity to get what I wanted whenever all else failed with my father.

But I was careful not to let my real self, that mentally sharp part of me be exposed. I did have one ally, however, who knew what I was up to. Every now and again she would step in and out-maneuver me, but it was her way of keeping me in check if I got too far out of hand and in danger of being exposed. Most of the time my mom would applaud my efforts, secretly enjoying my victories.

Being a girl limited me from going fishing and doing sports with my brothers since girls were supposed to learn how to cook, clean and sew. While sitting pretty with a dress on and keeping silent and still on a couch with company while they got to rip and run and laugh and play hide and seek.

There was the me that would smile and the me that would seethe. I did not really see it at the time as being the two faces of me until I made the mistake of unconsciously exposing myself to my dad one day when I was thirteen. I was just beginning my transition into being a young lady, and my mom was not there at the time. My hormones seemed to have a mind of their own and I could be emotionally expressive when I was not conscious of myself.

It was just this sort of situation that left me exposed that one day as my dad saw a side of my personality he did not like. Which prompted the words "You've got Hell in You."

It was those hurtful words that continued to haunt me throughout my adult life.

Now, Fast forward to my late forties...

My mom has just died. My dad and his now wife, who he, through the same manipulations he had always used had me calling her mom, lived in Florida.

I am unsettled by my mom's dying. There is a numbness that is running in my system from her leaving. I am angry with my brothers and dad and furious with how he is still running the show even though he is the one who left and moved away. And there are issues I've yet to expose and confront him on from my parent's divorce that only I know about.

This time Kali is not to be quieted or toned down.

On the night before my mom died, she came to me in a dream. She rang my doorbell, and when I opened the front door, there she stood – radiant and beautiful. I looked at her and asked her how this could be. I told her how beautiful she looked, and she told me. "The doctors fixed me" – her exact words. I said, "Well come inside," and she spoke. "I can't, I have things to do, people to see," and she turned around and walked down my front steps. I instantly woke up and thought: *Well, she is either dying or going to live* as I fell back to sleep and the dream faded. I had forgotten the dream when I woke up again that morning.

I got the call later that day that her time was up, and I had better come to the hospital now if I wanted to see her and say goodbye. After she had passed, I walked around trying to define what I was feeling. I was not sad because she had waited for me. And as I went over the dream again It felt like she had visited me. She never regained consciousness in the hospital, but I knew she heard me as I told her I loved her, and it was okay for her to go. She quietly left with a peaceful smile on her face as she took her last breath.

As I went home, I reflected on the dream again and wondered what it might have met as I remembered a similar time in my mom's life when my grandmother (her mother) had died. She had told me that she had a dream about her mom coming to see her too and then getting a call that evening that her mom had died. This became important to me, and it felt like there was something, some reason, that she had for coming to me in that way.

Over the next couple of days my dad and brothers closed ranks. My dad through emotional manipulation tried again to control the events surrounding my mom's funeral. But this time Kali was not in any mood to cooperate. She yelled and spoke to him and my brothers with truths that had been long held and buried, this surprised even me. But she was done. She was fed up and she was cleaning house. She was no longer the good girl's slave. No amount of shaming would change me. She just did not care anymore. All the pain and anger had finally been unleashed. It felt cleansing, Kali had finally roared.

After my tirade, I kept silent. I spoke to no one during the ceremony and left immediately afterwards to my dad's chagrin. He even tried to get my children to talk to me, but I refused to talk to them and kept silent with him and my brothers for 5 years. As I wrestled with the truth of what I had said, how I had spoken, how I had gone against the conditions and rules of respect for my elders that had been programmed in me for over 40 years, I felt no shame. Kali had unearthed righteous justification. I felt free and un-restrained for the first time in my life.

During that time, I went on a mission. I traveled back over my mom's life. I retraced her footsteps. I wanted to know the woman who raised me. I learned how strong-willed a person she was in her own quiet way and where that came from even though she had hidden a lot of it during her marriage. I learned how much she had endured as a dark-skinned person growing up in the south with a mother who looked white. And how she was treated as the

118

daughter of a preacher. I met her remaining relatives, friends, and ancestors. I learned the history of my mom's lineage and their Indigenous roots. I discovered that there were others who had similar dream experiences. It felt like I was on a pilgrimage, being led by my mother to the truth of who I am.

Those were my first deep dives of the many steps I was to take and am still making in my becoming. They were gifts that my mom left for me to find like buried treasure. I believe that her visit to me was her way of passing the torch over to me to continue or take up where she had left off on this human feminine journey of discovery. I was on a journey to discover me, to love me, to accept me, to empower me with my own brand of holy rage. And kali remains my ever-constant shadow companion who I have come to admire and trust. I claim her and I love her.

Trio of Kali Haikus

Nuit Moore

Surrendering to the Void,
my thunder echoes
divine lightning ebb and flow.

Surrendering as
the veil of illusion burns,
sacramental ash.

Maa whirlwind dervish
with fire and void thousand armed,
flow fierce radiance.

A Mirror on the Other Side

Diána Bósa

*"Some bright silhouette vision of a tiger
She's gonna eat through the other side of daylight."
(Public Memory – Midsummer Shadow)*∗

There is a mirror on the other side.

And I can feel it when she looks into it and reveals her face to that mirror.

For her gaze was the one that woke me up from my slumber. She has no idea that she has unfolded herself to me.

I am not lurking, though. The mirrors are just the shards of the black time, message carriers of this world's temporality. A mirror can be crushed or even destroyed but never the reflection.

She is coming closer now. Her movements are broken and stiff, somehow brittle. I can feel that she is in unendurable pain. After this world, her body also starts to betray her. Everything is leaving her on her own in this great fragility.

"Come here, my child," I say. "Let me have a look at you."

She obeys me, though she cannot hear my words—a pale young girl with long, blond hair. Only saw nineteen moons of her life. And now an incurable malady is feasting on her, chewing her mayfly life. It has already entirely deprived her of the years of blooming.

Yet still, I am aware that she is the one I was looking for. No matter her sick, dying body, her terrible loneliness in this world. Her rusty, ramshackle cage hides something precious, something vivid that she aims to overcome.

Her will to survive.

Her very heart.

She is standing in front of the mirror now, right before these eyes of mine. Her breathing becomes heavy as her lungs try to breathe in the last breath of air through the plastic pipes connected to the oxygen tank holder. She reminds me of myself now, as once upon a time, on a battlefield, I fiercely tried to suck all the blood of Raktabija.

She looks right into my eyes now, and I am impressed with her perseverance and relentlessness. She may lose this final battle in a long war for her life, but she will not give herself away so easily. She is determined to take a bite from the cruel End's heart – if there exists one. I smile.

Now she is mumbling something. One would think that's a prayer, a begging for her life. But it's not more like a vow that no one can wade through her. Not even Death.

"Let it be, Child. Just let it be. Or else, I cannot come to you."

She coughs heavily; her body slowly gives up.

I don't know how come she is still standing. What makes this tiny, birdy-bone girl stand on her feet though her strength is leaking from her body?

"But not her power; that won't leave her," I whisper, caressing her image in the mirror.

I am witnessing her last struggle as she collapses to the floor. With her final strength, she is tearing the plastic, already useless pipes from her nose. Not even an entire oxygen tank could save her now, only lengthening her suffering. And she is aware of this.

"Brave child. Now come, Death is not as terrible as it is said. You've already suffered too much."

Her lungs cannot serve enough air on their own to keep her weak body alive. She almost lost consciousness but still kept her eyes on the mirror. Not on her reflection, no. It is like, from now on, she is too capable of looking through it. And this gaze, the last one kissed by the road of passersby, is my portal. A door is finally left ajar between my world and hers.

I eat through the other side of daylight, sliding through easily this corridor between dimensions.

And through her dying gaze, I am flowing into her body.

From her body into her heart.

From her heart into her soul.

In the very moment of her agony, she welcomes me here. For she – already shaking off this life's hardnesses, deprived of her suffering, her memories, good and bad – recognizes me. She becomes imbued by me, both with my strength and my power. Her weak body is nothing to me: I can heal it easily by repairing it like a broken toy in the blink of an eye.

I will let her be herself, the one she was in the before-life. I only weave myself into her personality, but her appearance will remain the same.

Well, mostly. She does not need to wear my tiger skin sari or the garland of human heads.

But her skin will have a radiant blue shine, and yes, her feet and hands will preserve my touch with their blood color. And her sunken eyes will be red with intoxication and justified rage.

She will be a perfect host for me for that short period while I walk this Earth. For that time, I find Raktabija, whose blood seeds have already infected this world. The ones who wear his vile face. I will have to eradicate them, once and for all, by consuming every drop of blood that has ever dripped from Raktabija. I must make sure that no more demons can ever menace this kingdom.

And then, when I am done – because I will have everything done – there'll be only one thing left: having my last dance on the charnel ground.

Because I am here again.

Making it clearer, I have never left.

I am she who is red as the freshly dripped blood of women's wombs.

I am she who is blue as the dark night falling upon this world.

I am she who is black as the unquenchable Time.

I am Death blessing this Earth with my dancing feet.

I am Kali.

And nothing escapes from me.

*In the original lyrics, it appeared as 'He' and not 'She.'

A Prayer of Place (for Kali-Women)
Molly Remer

I hope you know a place
of holding,
a place of nourishing and unfolding.
I hope you know a place
where you belong,
where a thousand new stories
unfold every day,
and you're there,
seeing them,
a place where you are seen
and held
and heard,
a place of trust,
where you can grow
and change
and dance
and rage.
I hope you know a place
where you are part of the story,
where it is part of you
and you are part of it
and you belong with
and to and for each other.
I hope you know a place where
you can listen,
a place where you can learn,
a place where you can watch
the weaving of the world spin
and feel your place
within the very tapestry
of divinity itself.

Kali of the Torch Bearer
Kat Shaw

Kali: Time-Honored Teacher of Temperance

Dr. Denise Renye

Many folx have been culturally conditioned to shy away from both anger and the ability to demand what they want because they perceive both as "bad" or dangerous. Many people are told implicitly or explicitly to avoid even feeling angry or being demanding but I heartily disagree. Emotions are not good or bad, right or wrong. It's healthy to have awareness of anger because emotions show up for a reason. If you're angry and don't take it seriously and make room to feel it, you abandon yourself and send the message your feelings don't matter. In turn, you may displace your anger onto someone or something else without addressing the heart of the issue. Furthermore, when you do feel the displaced anger, it may burst forth with a vengeance even stronger than what you originally felt. Through the story of the goddess Kali, we can learn how anger is both necessary to create boundaries for the self to flourish and also how to have awareness of our relationship with anger so we do not get taken away by it in a too destructive way.

In addition to displacing anger, it can also be subverted and resurface as over- or undereating, misusing alcohol or other drugs, dissociating, bingeing TV or video games, or other self-sabotaging behaviors. In other words, by *not* expressing anger, you could be causing yourself more harm. Anger tends to turn inward when there is not a healthy expression outward. This is when depression or anxiety may rear their all too familiar heads.

I learned a lot about anger and what it can tell us when I was a clinical supervisor in an early intervention program in Philadelphia. At that time in my career and life, I went into families' homes who had children 3 years old and younger who were being evaluated for developmental delays. Anger showed up frequently in these families as they grappled with the fact their beloved child was potentially delayed developmentally. Kali, though known for embracing darkness and anger, is paradoxically a fierce protector through her deep motherly love. Just as the parents with whom I worked rose against any threat to their babies, Kali does the same for her eternal children. It's important to keep Kali's dual nature in mind because it demonstrates anger can be protective and nurturing. Maa Kaali, another spelling and name for Kali, being the fierce, protective mother that she is, also shows us how to take seriously and safeguard our own inner child/children and this is something each of us can benefit from learning.

In my role in Philadelphia at the time, I met with many families who in addition to receiving diagnoses for their children were also dealing with poverty, meaning they were contending with numerous, devastating blows. I mention this because as I supported them to the best of my ability by making space for their anger, and as we created that space together, we uncovered deep grief, loss, and sadness, which sometimes anger can mask. Yes, Kali expresses anger and goes on a bloody killing rampage in numerous stories, but she also has a deeply nurturing side. Anger can cut down what isn't working to make room for something new. Anger can be like a fire that sweeps through a dead forest creating space for new growth to prosper. If used constructively, anger can unearth so much and transform your life, as we see with the goddess Kali. Kali is the goddess of death and destruction, but also creation and salvation. These two go together: destruction and creation. For new life to spring forth, the old must be cleared away. Embracing death is a practice. Death is inevitable and by embracing the fact our physical bodies will all die; life can be that much richer. Kali, whose name means "she who is death" helps us see our shadow and embrace it. She is not afraid of entering into the darkness and she teaches us not to shy away from it either.

When anger shows up it's because a boundary has been crossed, a lie is being faced, or an injustice has occurred. Through Kali, we learn to use our voices when faced with an injustice. By voicing that boundary violation or injustice, then something new can arise. And through her, we learn to express that anger as well as move it through our bodies and come back to a state of homeostasis. Working with many folx, I have seen people struggle with anger, whether it's an inability to contain a temper or an inability to access it altogether. Kali and her infamous outrage teach us not to deny our experiences yet still have them authentically.

As much as I appreciate the power of anger, I also recognize feeling anger is very different from expressing it. Feeling anger is an internal process; it happens inside and can feel big and overwhelming at times. That's not the same as expressing anger, which can potentially result in harm to yourself, others, or inanimate objects, like your phone if you hurl it against a wall. I suggest taking a pause, which I know can be hard, but you can do it … with attention, breath, and practice! Kali was created from the goddess Durga with the specific task to express anger and take charge of a situation. Kali was expressing anger in a bloody murderous rampage, the divine feminine in full wrath. It was not until the divine masculine in the form of Shiva, her husband, showed himself to her (and she was dancing in glorious anger on top of him!) that she came to from her anger trance and paused. It is through her story that we can learn to dance with our anger and come to embrace it with temperance. The stories of the gods and goddesses (and stories such as fairytales) give us a view into the internal landscape and allow us to know different aspects of ourselves, such as the masculine and feminine energies that are alive in each of us. Shiva can be seen as representing the masculine, the energy within that assists with making boundaries and setting limits so as to keep us safe.

Two practices that may be helpful for you are yoga and movement meditation, which encourage you to notice the feelings and sensations in your body. These modalities can help raise awareness of anger, demand, resentment, or aggression in the body and also provide an outlet to move it around, out, and through. Raising awareness in and through the body helps to increase a sense of agency, gives confidence when creating or reestablishing a boundary, and own one's birthright of embodiment. If you can sit with the discomfort that often accompanies anger, and notice its multitude of nuances instead of exploding (or imploding through addiction or another form of self-harm) in the moment, it will create space and time for you to make decisions. The time and space would allow for responding instead of reacting. From that place, you can use anger constructively to do things like vote, protest, become aware of energetic boundaries that need to be in place, or have a boundary-setting conversation. That's not to say I recommend suppressing anger because I surely don't. Healthy ways of expressing it are stating out loud that you are feeling angry right now (this is advanced and needs to be practiced), screaming into a pillow, going for a run, dancing to angry music, sending letters and making calls to your governmental officials, attending protests, starting a revolution, venting to a friend or fellow, and journaling to name a few. There are more options than these, of course; the important thing is to find something that works for you. But once you do, your whole life can change and our society can change too. Anger gives you information about yourself and can allow you to take action in a way that is in alignment with your values at this given moment in time.

Kali is there in the depths of the hearts of people who have no voice. She is waiting to be summoned. She is there behind the eyes of the victimized. She is waiting to be unleashed. However, the wrath of Maa Kaali must be revered and honored deeply for it could become chaos in its own right. Without awareness, the destructive forces of anger can kill the innocent.

We are all dancing that fine line between too much and too little in this lifetime. If you'd like support accessing your inner Kali in a healthy way, as a yoga therapist, I recommend pairing the asana Goddess pose with Lion's breath meditation.

Utkata Konasana (Goddess Pose) invites you to take up all the space you need. The pose opens the hips and increases the range of motion in the hips and pelvis. The name of the pose stems from the Sanskrit word *Utkata*, which means powerful or fierce, and *Kona*, which means angle. The pose is said to have originated from Kali, so that's why it's called Goddess Pose, Victory Squat Pose, or *Deviasana/Kaliasana*.

Once you're in *Utkata Konasana*, you can start Lion's breath meditation. Open your mouth wide and stick out your tongue, like in the many depictions of Kali. Stretch it as far as you can to your chin. Exhale forcefully so your breath crosses the base of your tongue. As you're exhaling, make a "ha" sound from deep within your abdomen. Then breathe normally for a few moments. By acknowledging anger and doing practices to move it through the body, you aren't keeping the angry energy trapped. It doesn't stagnate and turn into a larger problem later. Instead, you're using anger in a healthy, transformative way, which can be fuel to power positive change. And that's something we could all use a little more of.

If Kali Was My Muse

Rhonda Melanson

she'd demand India ink for permanence and colour
order a violent shakedown of my dainty pen, dare me
to guess the demon-shaped puddle splattered there
        on anxiety-toned white

what do you think that inkblot means?

Put it on heat, ask it to tea- together read its rotted leaves

write a sonnet with its ink.

Might I someday ghost-write her gospel?

Kali Rising
Louise Cox

Fearless Kali

Louise Cox

When all else fails and even the Gods cannot defeat the Demons it is Kali who is called upon. The world is ripe for a Kali rising. We have contained our rage for long enough. Inevitably, like a volcano, it will erupt a fiery wrath.

As I write this, I too call to Kali. I feel her searing hot rage course through my body, igniting sparks as it goes.

I could easily destroy the world around me and have done this many times. For once Kali is dancing in blind fury, it's hard to know when to stop. But I am older now... When you are young, total destruction is not so bad – you have time to rebuild your world. Sometimes this process is needed to start again, reborn. I no longer have the luxury of time left in this life. I am learning that I, like Kali, need Shiva to calm me before all existence is obliterated. I, too, need to cultivate a calm eye within the tempest of my rage so that only the Demons are destroyed and not the whole of my world along with it.

My mind kept returning to an encounter with Shiva and I kept putting it to one side. This is a book about Kali, but my mind was insistent and then I came to a realisation. Reacquainting myself with some of my favourite books on Kali, there are parallels between stories of Kali and my encounter with Shiva. I still keep dismissing it, it's out of context! Finally, I listen to my inner voice as it is insistent that this is what I should write.

Here is my story.

On night of the millennium 2000, Shiva appeared to me in a Dream. This was no ordinary dream. I had been preparing myself for a month to have a Vision of Krishna in my Dreams. On that night as we entered a new era, I did not have a Vision of Krishna.

In the dream I was in a museum looking at a table covered in beautiful statues of deities. I was drawn to a statue of Shiva carved out of red stone. Moving closer to take in the intricate details of the carving, I was instantly transported onto a battlefield. A fierce and brutal battle was fought that night. I was fearless; when the battle was over the corpses of the dead lay slain around me. I was overwhelmed with sadness and mourned for the dead and the futility of war. Then, remembering words from The Bhagavad-Gita, I understood Krishna's words on life, death, and the indestructible nature of soul to Arjuna at that moment with such clarity the universe expanded before me.[14]

Now back in the museum, I knelt in front of the statue of Shiva to thank him for this enlightenment. Kneeling face down in prayer, I felt someone stand over me, feet planted either side of my body holding me tightly so I could not escape. Sensing this immensely powerful being standing directly over my small curled up frame, pressing against my thighs so tightly I might be crushed. I Knew it was Shiva. Still fearless, I dared to open my eyes just a crack at first. I could see Shiva's skirt swaying above my head, flayed tiger skin and black ropes brushed my hair. Summoning courage I braved to turn my face and look up to Shiva, as I did, he bent down towards me and licked my face.

Hence, I accepted that I am not of the light of Krishna, I am of the darkness Shiva.

On the 2nd of January 2000, I was attacked on the way home from work. Let's just say the attacker was not interested in the contents of my purse. I remained calm throughout the attack, fought the attacker off, and he only left with bruised balls.

I believe the dream helped me to stay calm, not be afraid, and was some sort of lesson to ready me for what was to come.

---

[14] Bhagavad-Gita 2:7-9 (Johnson W. J., The Bhagavad-Gita – A new translation.

I had always put the emphasis on Shiva, as it was Shiva who appeared to me in my Dream.

Looking back with fresh eyes, I was struck with the realisation that you cannot have one without the other Kali and Shiva are intertwined.

Considering my belief has always centred around the union of male and female as one – a union of god and goddess within us – I don't know why the revelation of this dream has only just hit.[15]

Shiva was the calm before and after the battle. The fearless warrior in me that fought the battle was Kali. Just like the battle myths of Kali.[16]

It was Kali who gave me the inner strength that night in the dream and then in the face of my attacker. I had faced one of my darkest fears – and my inner goddess that was fearless was Kali.

After the attack my whole attitude became fearless. By 2003 I had ended the relationship I was in, started my own business and bought my first home. I was that fearless goddess.

Somewhere along the way I lost her, but she is reawakening. Every day I feel her, the kundalini snake in my belly uncoils and stretches a little in readiness.

Back to the present day 2022 and the current turmoil in my life evokes the rage of Kali once more. I need the calm hand of Shiva to stop me in my tracks. As he stops Kali in the field of battle, and she realises she is about to kill her husband and the destroy the entire universe along with the Demons. I too need to stop and take a calm look at the situation before me.

---

[15] "Shiva cannot personify himself without Shakti", Harding E. Kali – The black goddess of Dakshinewar; p 158. "Kali cannot exist without him, and Shiva cannot reveal himself without her", Harding E. Kali – The black goddess of Dakshinewar; p 41.
[16] Kinsley D. Hindu Goddesses – Vision of the divine feminine in the Hindu tradition; p 118.

Justified rage is acceptable but we must all learn to stop before we destroy what we love along with the Demons – whether that is within ourselves or as a society at large.

Therefore remember…

We are fierce Goddesses. When you look at your reflection in the mirror, see the Goddess stare back at you. Be outraged but don't lose sight or burn bridges. Set the world alight if you must, but don't self-destruct in the process. Keep an eye of calm in your tempest of rage. Be both the fearless goddess Kali and the calm clarity of Shiva within.

Kali
Louise Cox

Kali Coloring Sheet
Louise Cox

The Cosmic Dance

Barbara O'Meara

With you our great Cosmic Mother we step into the dance
With the vision of your third eye, we move and we chant
You who embody in all living beings the feminine mystique
Gift us righteousness and bravery to become women unique
We honor and hold your rich symbols in the highest esteem
Our spirits release that which no longer serves you
Oh Powerful Queen
Guided by you, Kali, we ferociously discover
That the Celestial Cosmos is now ours to recover

We become new Cosmic Dancers with movements
pulsating and wild
Rising and writhing of round bellies and abundant thighs
Hips, wombs and yonis all gyrating and snaking
Manifesting your essence of truth, without any faking
Our uplifted energies are held in the salvation of your Yonic Pose
Resurgence and restoration, over time and true nature, grows
Guided by you, Kalika Mai, we sublimely discover
That the Celestial Cosmos is now ours to recover

In divine elevation we are alive and strong with sacred rage
We stick out our raw crimson tongues
as your anger we now gauge
We hiss when we gesture, we no longer need to behave well
We caress our bodies with divine Kali
markings of which we have heard tell
A tribute to our bleeding, our birthing, and our womanly love
Be-shrouded in smoky mysteries
that you have bestowed from above
Guided by you, Badra Kali, we infinitely discover
That the Celestial Cosmos is now ours to recover

Our dance moves in timelessness as many skins we must shed
Elemental touchstones allow us to give up our dead
We honor the light and freedom that you bring into our lives
We move reverently to your rhythms,
Creatrix, who has eternally survived
Primordial source of all life, manifestor of innocence,
destroyer of evil
We righteously claim your name no matter what the upheaval
Guided by you Mother Kali we compassionately discover
That the Celestial Cosmos is now ours to recover

We embrace your ferocious power, your vital salvation
Swaying to cycles of change,
guided by you Dark Mother of Creation
We sever all ties with ego and ignorance,
all eternal struggles we abandon
Universally our bodies move in synchronicity,
no forward step in now random
We sound your name Kali Mata
with limitless surety and by design
All knowing within, we are no longer complacent,
powerless or benign
Guided by you, our Great Cosmic Mother we blissfully discover
That the Celestial Cosmos is now ours to recover

Barbara O'Meara August 2022

The Cosmic Dance with Kali
Barbara O'Meara

Unraveled

Hanna Verge

Words have taken on new meaning and symbols have come to make sense in a way they never have before. *My heart is on fire.* Kali has placed her foot on my chest and all that I once was is burning away. I can feel it, like a hot lump of coal, all the darkness will be burned away to the point of what? Will anything remain? I like the idea of revealing a big diamond or other shiny gem to prove my heart is valuable. But then what about annihilation? All signs are pointing to the idea that "I" will cease to be.

While "I" am being burned up, I need to open my mouth and let my tongue hang out to let the heat escape. I can feel my eyes become wild, while my vision becomes fierce and sharp.

Sometimes it scares my husband.

"Are you okay? You look crazed," he said behind his own wide eyes.

Once upon a time, I might have questioned it. Was I okay? Am I imagining things? Can I go through this spiritual transformation and not be crazy, not *lose control?* For a few months there I was afraid I might be developing a severe mental illness.

I am a licensed mental health counselor after all.

I was fed sterile conclusions of clinical expertise and diagnoses, but not all therapists have been like this. And so, I follow Carl Jung, and know that I am not alone. What I went through, and I hope never stops, was real, and *is real.* Sure, it has not yet been measured or examined by human hands in clean white labs or through wires attached to my skull, but that doesn't mean it isn't happening. That doesn't mean the collective unconscious is not a well of poetry, that can be lived through each individual soul in whatever way it has come to express itself this time around.

In the end, people can call my inner life whatever they wish. I don't really care because what do they know and what does it matter? I am my own individual person. Having my own experiences, and my understanding is what matters most to me. I get to choose what I believe or not, what I do or not, who I listen to or not, and who I speak to or not. I get to choose what sits well in my fire, and know that diagnosing it is beside the point. It is elusive and expansive, and constantly changing, while something within me is completely still and eternal. I have come to know this raging hot change as Kali.

I can feel Her dancing through me, as me, for she is me, and I am Her. I imagine in some realm, somewhere, I am small, about the size of a mouse, hugging onto her huge cosmic arm and she welcomes me and lets me rest in her lap. Though I think that is someone "else" entirely.

In my life though, this one where I am a human on this planet, I want to be here in this fire as I dance my way through life. I will not abandon the world as I've long wanted to, because the confusion and pain was all too much. But I don't feel so confused anymore. In fact, I feel more sane and awake than ever, but this doesn't mean I am some Holy Ghost that floats through life in a constant state of purity and joy. Because at times, when I am mistreated, I do feel sort of crazed, like Kali ripping off heads and killing all the illusions of who I am, and how I am meant to be treated, or even still, how I am "meant" to act. Only now I don't have to feel bad about it. I don't need to feel ashamed of my anger, for I am not out to hurt anyone. In that way, I exercise control and know that I am okay. Sometimes anger is righteous and standing up for yourself is the best thing you can do.

As for the people who don't like it when I assert myself, who have called my raised voice against their manipulative head games "abusive," well they're my oppressors. There is no more pulling the wool over my eyes. Psychological and emotional abuse is real and it is far more common than I have ever realized. My

144

retaliation against it is reactive abuse, which is an insidious tactic that abusers use to spin the table on the victim, leaving them ashamed and guilty. It manipulates the victim into thinking, believing, and questioning if they are the abusive one. It is wrong. It is so wrong, and whether the abuser knows what they're doing or not, it remains wrong.

The truth is, people have hurt me, deeply. People have hurt me and twisted it around. They have put the guilt and shame on me. People have violated me, and I was taught to ignore it. Little Hanna was *molested* by her paternal grandfather and she told the nearest trusted adult after it was all over. The adult stuttered and muttered excuses, and I was told to keep it quiet. Talk about Holy Rage. And this is only one experience. I'm sure you can guess the rest; betrayals, lies, crazy-making, guilt-tripping, gas-lighting, put-downs, and cruel comparisons. You name it. People that I trusted and were supposed to protect me and have my back, have messed with my confused little head, until now.

Now I call it by its right name: Abuse.

This is my Holy Rage, where I stand strong in what is right and wrong, black and white, clear-cut, no shades of gray. I've crossed the ancient bridge over shallow water and found myself in the cave, where the walls are painted with bright magenta and shimmering pink, and I am an artist, here to help abused women and children see the light. I am here to guide them through Kali's battlefield as all of their perceptions are dropped, leaving them rattled and confused. I promise them, they're on their way. They're getting better. It *is* hard. I use myself as a beacon in the night to prove that it is all real and people can get better, and be better than the people who have hurt them. Though I keep this all to myself, like a little secret, as I stand atop the tower and look far and wide into the past and potential future of my clients.

I feel it is important to talk about men as well, for they can be abused too. I have a male client as I write this, who is mentally abused by his wife, only I don't think he is a man. Not in those moments. To me, I see him as a child trapped in a man's body. He has not entered his true masculinity just yet. He is stunted by childhood trauma and abuses of his own, now being played out again with his wife, who incessantly picks at his delicate psyche and sensitive heart. I stoke his flame and let him know his anger has a place. I tell him it's okay to tell her to "stop," and let him know that if she doesn't, it's okay for him to leave. No one would blame him if they knew his Truth.

In this way, I see us all on this journey together. The dysfunction that happened in our childhoods and families, up until whatever point our perceptive shifts, is never a true reflection of reality. It is distorted and sick, designed to maintain a hierarchy, only hierarchies are not the way human beings connect. It is not love. We love one another on the battlefield, whooping and cheering one another on, as our own individual realities are shattered. Or we stand on the sidelines, smiling and nodding, knowing what it is. Nothing is what we think it is, it is so much more.

As for me, I can say this; while I would not wish what happened to me on anyone, I now see it as the place of opening. My Truth is the light for others now, just as other's Truths have been the light for me. I know that I would not be where I am today if it was not for the work I did with a client who hammered little bits of her sexual abuse into each and every session. Her Truth opened me to mine, and it was not pretty.

I unraveled. I could feel the tuft of yarn hanging from my skull and I was afraid to pull it, because I didn't know what would happen if I did. I was afraid I'd cease to exist. And I have, in a way. Only, that pure point of eternal being has remained, and all the excess fluff and entanglement has dropped. I ceased to exist as I once was, and I'm so glad that it happened. Even back then, I didn't know it yet, but Kali was blessing my life.

One dark winter morning I sat alone in meditation, in the solitude of my living room. I sat in the swirl of my unraveling, shaken but not lost. My four-year-old son did not yet lift his head from his pillow and my husband stayed cuddled under our blankets. It was in the first weeks of being in therapy of my own, recovering from alcohol abuse, depression, and toxic entanglements, when some dark woman came dancing into my mind's eye. I didn't know who she was, but I liked her. She was kind of funny, the way she danced on her tip toes, with her red tongue hanging out of her mouth, because she'd stop and check, to be sure I was watching. It was amusing and pure, even though it was not what society would say is acceptable. Her breasts were bare, her hair was wild and untamed, she was barefoot, and her skin was so dark that it shimmered gold and silver. Above all, she had no shame. Not an ounce of it.

How could I have been so blessed?

Kali the Slayer
Kat Shaw

KALI, Mother of Annihilation

Carrie Kopp Adams

My story with Kali is ever ongoing.

Once you open up a relationship with her, it doesn't stop.

If you agree to the process of shedding your demons, you agree to let her liberate you for life.

I am a massage therapist by trade, yoga instructor & wellness coach.

I don't often speak to my clients about my spiritual experiences, as most of them are recovering from illness or injury and subscribe to a more tangible way of looking at things.

But, as my practice evolves, I find that energy medicine plays an integral role in good health, and we as individuals can increase our vitality by aligning with nature and asking our healing guides for help.

At one such point, I turned to Kali.

She had been ever-present at my door, inserting herself into my purview in various ways. I resisted praying to her as my yogic texts suggested she was a goddess of destruction – and certainly, her imagery evoked a certain kind of violence.

Movies like Indiana Jones and the Temple of Doom only re-enforced this idea; perhaps, inspired by the wrongful demonization of some of her followers.

Yet, in my experience, Kali came as a divine mother, and her process was that of a gentle cleanse.

I was having trouble sleeping and I wanted radical change – and this she brought me almost instantly.

When I thought the work was done, she found me out walking and reminded me the true work had only begun.

Floating beside me as a maiden, she occasionally flashed her blue face at cars speeding down the street, tongue wagging. When I asked her what the mission was, she replied, " To not seek to constantly see the demons of others as I do."

It was permission to look critically at myself instead of everyone else.

A karmic detox followed, forcing me to radically change my diet. In doing so, I connected with the ancestors, who knew food at its bare taste. I stopped craving excess, sauces, and sugar. My gut healed, my hair grew thicker and my eyes brighter.

Kali helped me reach a new level of personal sovereignty by showing me how to feel grounded in my body. She empowered me to prioritize simplicity and balance the desire for pleasure. I reclaimed the power to choose, to govern myself and achieve real peace.

Kali is a great awakener through annihilation. She shows us that one form must die in order to give birth to another. She brings us back to our senses through the shattering of the ego.

But she is not a goddess to be trifled with or ignored. Her holy rage may be turned, I have heard, on the uncommitted. It would be wise to seek her assistance only when you are sure it's what you want, and when you are prepared for total transformation.

I Will Destroy You
Stella Tomlinson

I hear you invoking me.
Kali. Dark Mother. Destroyer.
Life – Death – Rebirth Goddess.

But can you handle me, girl?
I will come and burn and sever and destroy,
I will pull down all that you have built on shaky foundations.

Am I not what you were asking for?
Do you want to be coddled and comforted and soothed?
Are you a girl who wants her mummy?
Or are you a woman ready to embody fierce rage?

For I will cut through your bullshit, and pretence,
And all that you think you hold dear.
It will feel like you are dying.

Hear the flash of my blades,
Feel the edifices crumbling,
Inhale the scent of burning.

I will destroy you.

And in your death
I will hold you
And rebirth you
As the powerful woman you truly are.

Her Ravenous Assumption

Jenn Martinez

It is I, Kali

Lily Munroe

It is I, Kali. I come before you in my vibrational dance. I enter your field with the grandeur of earth and stars coalesced. The great primordial mother, She of ten thousand names, the beginning and the end. I am the All, the everything. I am dark space, the galaxies, the planets, and the flesh. I am the creator and the destroyer. I am the dark moon and the full, the fall and the spring. I am the mighty She that stands at the conception and cessation of all worlds, the great regeneratrix, guiding my daughters to strength and fruition, passion and power, peace, and destiny.

When I appear I bring death to all that has had its time, as we writhe together in a fusion of love and holy rage, birthing anew onto pathways of fateful beginnings; beginnings formed in my hallowed womb, Dark Mother, Kali-Ma. I am She from before time, She of no time, shakti, dharma, forever's familiar, star of stars. I am the universe, the one-song, the female divine. I am She who rises against injustice, severing tethers of control, slayer of domination. Liberating my daughters from the bridle, sanctifying the sacred blood of your cycle; blessed life-givers of physicality and invention, I honour thee from dusk 'til dawn. I am the truth laid bare as bones.

I greet my daughters gently when I come, as some may fear my presence, at first; the sensation of my raw life-force energy, unknown to them for too long in a narrative ruled by men. For patriarchy has wielded the power to hide, distort, deny, the true essence of Goddess in our many guises, so that our depths, our vastness, our superb cosmic mysteries seem unfamiliar, at first. But Goddess can never be suppressed. I greet my daughters gently, so they know my primal power is life sparked in love.

And I proclaim, I am here, beloveds, call my mighty name, to clear and cleanse and close the doors of that which no longer serves, of that which inters, to release what has a hold, of all that scolds. And I promise – my eternal promise – that on the closing of the past, on the bodies of the dead, I always spawn the fresh bloom of the new flower you shall become. For I am the creatrix at my daughter's side, her kin in this journey of humanity, of sensory touch, taste, smell, of sight and sound, of mind and will, of expansion and artistry, of all the deliciousness that life brings, of all you revel in – oh, how I delight in witnessing this majesty, the majesty of you, the magic you brew.

So, I guide you, daughters, to speak my sacred name, at any hour, in any place. To embody your legacy as the female of old, of She who has become, of She who has come forth on this earth as one from the cauldron of everything. And I shall emerge, flowing like great rivers of blood that course through your veins, that fill your womb and shed from your yoni, as you slip through the veils like only She can, opening portals through your wild body, your activating hands, your bold heart and mind. My lineage divine. My lineage in flesh, expressed.

I am here also, my loves, to ignite and spin throat chakras blue, to enable the voices of women across the globe, to speak with wisdom and power, with freedom and solutions, to speak up for herself and her sisters too. To speak of the wrongs that have tried to silence her, to speak of the truths that she knows of inside her, for she has the mighty Kali-Ma beside her, with my vow of new life, and, though it may seem so at times, my vow that none shall bear the life-death-life cycles alone.

Know that even in my rage with your rage, of what has befallen you, I am here in pure love, always, in all ways. A being who can hold polarities all at once. I swathe the fury of inequality while holding the circle to release, reweave, reclaim; where violations are evinced, and tunes of rebirth are sung. I dance my dance through your bodies and shake the ground beneath your feet, to unburden, to align, so your centre you may once again find. So, dance with me, daughters, dance with me, dance.

As you purge from your body, with movement like waves, breathe out ghosts that haunt with my sigh untamed. May your tongue protrude fierce like mine, unrestrained, as I move worlds within you, transmuted, with new aim. For your wilderness it craves, sacred reunion, codes of revolution, an initiation of remembering that reinvigorates your path. Feel it, feel it now, in cells, in blood, in belly fire, in heart, and know that I have come. Know my presence as you sense a shimmering blue of wonderment, a coolness and heat at the same time, a strength inside unruly love, and by my mighty breath – *Haaaahhhh!* It is I, Kali.

Shadow Work
Erika Lopp

My Fury is transformative. My sword drips with the blood of my enemies, vanquished by my wrath. Do not fear what lies within you. Take my hand and I will walk with you through perdition, to the other side where perfect peace dwells. I hold the key. I will unlock the door, beyond the veil of your mind. Walk through this door. Your journey begins with an ending. A painful bittersweet conclusion to the self you were before. Personal growth is the greatest of battles, a liberation worth immense suffering. Step into my shadow and I will reveal your light. My hourglass sets on the altar of time, renewal, and creation, begotten only by destruction and blood. Realize I am Nature. I am the force that purges all things. I am kind and ruthless, loving, and vengeful. I am the Divine Mother and the Warrior Wraith. All things pass through me. Time is my dearest friend. I exist beyond it and before it. I am the artist of shadows, dressed in the thought forms of the pure and wicked alike. Do not fear me, for it is I who should fear you. Together we will conquer the demons that plague your mind. I am a worthy ally. Find me in the void. Call my name Kali Ma. In the darkness, I shall bring you salvation.

Prayer to Kali Ma

Kali Ma, Mother of Darkness, I ask for your guidance. Help me to better know myself. Be the mirror that reflects my shadows. Hold my hand during this painful personal journey. Lend me your strength. May I not fear my own darkness and embrace my truest self. With blessings and reverence, I ask your aid.

Dark Mother Divine

Shalini Angela Persaud

The darkness of your love radiates
Alive and pulsing
      Strong and persisting
Sweet siren
Seducing, embracing, leading...

Mother Kali... your dark love embraced me
When I called and you answered
Saviour and protector
Avenger and destroyer
In your power and darkness
I find true love and beauty
Never found in this world

Dance for me, Goddess
In wild, untamed frenzy
Let me hear the bells on your feet
And the beat of the drums
Sweep me off my feet
Like a crazy hurricane

Let me rise like a phoenix
Amidst the destruction of your creation
Let me fly like a dragon
From the ashes... with you
Renewed, recreated, alive
Empowered, strengthened
By your eternal love
In the darkness of my soul.

Kali II
Michelle Moirai

RAGE. RAGE? RAGE!!

C. Ara Campbell

What do we imagine when we think of the fierce aspects of the Goddess? Is She enraged? Destructive? Do we shy away from Her power? Do we avert our gaze from Her wild eyes and bloody teeth fresh from battle?

We have been taught that the fiery aspects of the divine feminine need to be suppressed, along with our own ferocious nature. The toxic patriarchy loves nothing more than to paint the fearsome feminine forces as evil. Kali is no different. We share Her fate being told we are too passionate, too loud, too angry. What a load of bullshit. The patriarchy fears the fire breathing Goddesses you see. For She will burn their outdated paradigms to ash.

Kali is the destroyer of these old structures, for She is the embodiment of justified rage. She shows us the need to connect with the inferno within and embrace the fury that wells in our outraged souls at the injustices of the world. She teaches us that sometimes things get messy, dirty, and covered in blood, as we chase down the demons in our own lives.

She calls to us to riot against the obsolete illusions, rules, and definitions that society would bind us with. Through Kali, we cut the strings the puppet masters would use upon us, and we incinerate their delusions of enslavement and subjugation to the ground. She calls to us to rise, sword in hand, and stand against the storm of corruption that would consume us all. Our rage is justified, She growls. Our fight is just.

The Goddess Kali has surged strongly in my veins my whole life, whether I knew Her name yet or not. I was a firebrand, passionate towards all causes just, defiant in the face of tyranny and oppression. As a child, my mother affectionately nicknamed me Spitfire, recognizing the blaze that burned within me, my desire to be both righteous sword and protective shield. There didn't seem to be a day that went by where I wasn't championing some cause or another, be it the rights of animals, the absurdity of the bible or the ridiculous way society wanted little girls to dress and behave. She saw it too and told my sister and I the importance of standing up for ourselves when others would push their wills and biases upon us. *"If they start the fight, you finish it,"* she would say. So, I did.

One day when I was in kindergarten, I was playing on the playground with fellow children in my class. We were having fun on a large snow hill sliding down in a haze of laughter and charging back up to the top to do it again.

However, the fun was cut short. The older kids in grade 6 had begun to push the little kindergarten children off the snow hill, claiming it as their own. The children were sad and disappointed, defeated by the bullies.

Something feral thundered inside me. Justified rage, the primal need to devour all the demons to make the world safe again. Tiny human that I was at the age of 5, I was enflamed. This isn't right, the hellfire within me roared.

I raged against those who would harm and bully others. I raged at the injustice of it with a purity found in the heart of one so young. How dare they? Who did they think they were? Why did they think they had the authority to take something away from another? So, I raged. Roaring, pushing them away, wrestling them all the way down the snow hill and right into the principal's office.

I stood accused of fighting; the reason why was unimportant to the adults. The powers that be wanted to punish me for my justified rage, for the flames that ignited my soul. They would prefer me to be an accepting drone following orders than to stand up and rally against injustice. I should have called a teacher instead of taking matters into my own hands. This is what they tried to instill upon me. Obedience. Silence. Complacency. Submission. Train the children to be digestible, good little beings that did as they were told and behaved properly.

And they failed miserably.

This wasn't about fitting in at school or being a "good kid." They had been brainwashed to crush our rebellious spirits and extinguish our fire just as society had done to them when they were children. The powers that be tried to dull the anger out of us, cut away the justified rage and replace it with being nice and proper. If we are watered down and silent, who would stand against their tyranny and push back against their oppression?

Fuck that. Let them keep their chains of propriety. Their punishment did nothing to suffocate the wildfire that welled in my being. Speaking out against injustice is a blade I continue to wield to this day.

Kali is a gateway to the justified rage that we have been taught to silence, the embodiment of the anger we have been programmed to swallow. Our connection to the Goddess Kali emboldens us with the courage needed to fight for what's right and for our own truth. To stand up to the injustices of the world and face those who would take it all from us. Our choices, our dreams, our bodies, our future, our very lives.

Within the pages of this anthology, we experience the courageous beating hearts of fierce souls raising their voices in a collective battle cry from across the globe. The howls of Kali's army screaming we will not surrender. We will not bow. We will not break.

To those who are fighting for their freedom, we stand with you, in any way that we can. We see and honor your battle and tell your stories. We honor your truth, your bravery, and your courageous spirit. Like the Goddess Kali, you combat the demons of our time. We raise our swords with you.

And so, we rage. To Kali, we call, our cries rising. The time has come. We cannot and will not go back. We fight for justice, for freedom, and for our rights. We stand with those that the patriarchy would tether and silence.

We will not be subjugated. We will not be erased. We will not go gentle. We will not back down. We will not be silent when war is waged upon our very existence.

As my mother said, *"If they start the fight, you finish it."*

And so, we shall.

List of Contributors

Andrea Ayla Sib is a modern priestess who initiates both women and men into womb mysteries – secrets of Holy Grail. She guides women on the path of embracing their own femininity through reconnecting with the natural rhythm of their lunar cycle, re-remembering the wisdom of sacred menstrual blood and magic of sacred sexuality.

Angie McCourt is an Author, *Host of Shifting Inside Out* Podcast and Founder, Success + Mindset Coach of Authentic Me Revolution. She shifted from a 27-year career as a successful business leader into the helping industry at a time where major change can happen, including revolutionizing the workplace and life in general. As a Career Success + Mindset Coach she helps clients shift their limiting beliefs and discover their elevated gifts so they can show up as their true self. She is an integrative certified Success Coach and Master NLP, EFT, Vitality, TIME Techniques and Hypnotherapy practitioner.

Her first published book is titled *Love Your Gifts: Permission to Revolutionize Authenticity in the Workplace.* Angie's mission is to help others discover their gifts, be true to their self and find joy through mindset shift and actions to create the life they want to live.

Barbara O'Meara (April 11th, 1963 – October 5th, 2023) was a professional visual artist, art activist, published writer & co-editor of *Soul Seers Irish Anthology of Celtic Shamanism.* Her 20 Solo Exhibitions included 'B.O.R.N. Babies of Ravaged Nations'. International juried shows include ASWM 'Wisdom Across the Ages', Lockhart Gallery New York 'Contemporary Irish Art' & Herstory 'Brigid's of the World' & 'Black Lives Matter'. Community Arts include 'Stitched With Love' Tuam Baby Blanket laid out onsite at the Mother & Child Institution by survivors and families, at KOLO International Women's Non Killing Cross Borders Summit in Sarajevo and held by Bosnian women war survivors. 'Sort Our Smears' Campaign at 'Festival of FeminismS'. 'Home Words Bound' publication with National Collective of Community Based Women's Networks where her paintings accompany writing by Irish women about the Pandemic. She continually developed empowering women's 'Art as Activism' projects through her final weeks. She was honoured to be featured in many Girl God Books and was the selected artist of *My Name is Brigid,* which launched on Brigid's Day 2022.

Barbara passed peacefully in the care of her beloved family on October 5th, 2023. She was in the midst of compiling *Sacred Breasts: an Inspirational Anthology for Living Your Breast Life.* The anthology will be completed and published in her honor by her co-editors. Her longtime sister-friend Dr. Karen Ward stepped up in her place to join the editing team. A follow up anthology about Brigid is also in the works in her memory. www.barbaraomearaartist.com

Bobbye Middendorf, MA, is dedicated to dreaming in new realities — where all life flourishes. She partners with Evolutionaries resonating with her #HeartFireMagic, spoken word alchemy, & sacred medicine. Her healing, creative, & alchemical transmissions offer portals for immersing in wisdom, grace, creative sparks, & self-love.

As Inner Wisdom Guide, she is devoted to each Beloved's blossoming from within... a magical journey available to all!

As Beacon & Word Alchemist, she delights in playing with poets, radiant edge-dwellers, goddesses, mystic witches, & creators — amplifying all these lights.

As Living Bridge between worlds, Bobbye's multidimensional work, including "Word Altar" collages + poetry, prompts playmates to remember their wisdom embodied within.

A WayMaker for WayMakers, Bobbye Co-Creates gatherings, dream groups, seasonal circles, pollination projects, mixed media collages, poems, prayers, & new realities. Those called to play in her #YinArising field can open to receive & live their bigger stories — healing, evolving, creating, & growing their embodied magic.

C. Ara Campbell is the author of the book *Dark Goddess Magick*, and founder of *The Goddess Circle*. She's a soul-guide, facilitator of *The Inner Priestess Awakening Online Journey* and *Relationship Empowerment & Sacred Love Online Journey,* and author of *The Astro Forecast Publication*. She is a contributing author on *Journeys with the Divine Feminine, Original Resistance: Reclaiming Lilith, Reclaiming Ourselves*, and contributing author and editor on *Kali Rising, Holy Rage*. Ara is a modern-day mystic dedicated to empowering others, connecting them with their purpose, living embodied truth and healing using the natural world. Ara is an old soul that has been writing and channeling cosmic guidance from the unseen since she was young, intuitively soul coaching using spiritual and natural energies. She can often be found seeking wisdom and solace in the wilds of Mother Earth, capturing the magic of nature with her camera, or snuggling her dog, Sonny.

Carrie Kopp Adams is a massage therapist, yoga instructor & wellness coach. She is the founder of www.massage-by-carrie.com, a mobile wellness company. Find her on Youtube @tarotbycarrie for free tarot readings, guided meditations, and reiki healing sessions.

Claire Dorey
Goldsmiths: BA Hons Fine Art.
Main Employment: Journalist and Creative, UK and overseas.
Artist: Most notable group show; *Pillow Talk* at the Tate Modern. Included in the *Pillow Talk* Book.

Curator: 3 x grass roots SLWA exhibitions and educational events on the subject of Female Empowerment, showcasing female artists, academic speeches, and local musicians. Silence Is Over – Raising awareness on violence towards women; Ex Voto – Existential Mexican Art Therapy; Heo – Female empowerment in the self-portrait.

Extra study: Suppressed Female History: History of the Goddess; Accessing Creative Wisdom; Sound and Breath Work; Reiki Master; Colour Therapy; Hand Mudras; Reflexology; Sculpture. Teaching Workshops: Sculpture and Drawing.

Deborah A. Meyerriecks learned to grow with Goddess and Thrive, not just merely survive. The newest title spontaneously bestowed on her which she carries with gratitude and received with love is 'Spiritual EMT.' A retired NYC*EMS career EMT and FDNY EMS Field Lieutenant, Deborah spent a lifetime being a voice for others who would be silenced as she had been before she learned that Holy Rage burns when it's not released for growth and protection. Deborah is the author of *Macha and the Medic*, a contributing author in *Prayers To The Morrigan* and Girl God Books: *Warrior Queen, Just As I Am*, and *Re-Membering with Goddess*. Deborah works to empower others though Shadow Work and more importantly, Shadow Care. She offers one-on-one Spiritual Counseling and Shadow Care Retreat weekends to facilitate others to do their own work with guidance and support. Find her through her author page on Facebook and at www.WillowMoon.com.

Dr. Denise Renye is a licensed clinical psychologist, certified sexologist, consultant and holistic coach, certified yoga therapist, and psychedelic integrationist. She has specialized training in and has worked directly with people in the areas of sexuality, relationships, embodiment, states of consciousness, psychedelic integration, and intimacy. She holds a Master's degree in Human Sexuality from Widener University (Philadelphia), as well as a Master's degree and a Doctoral degree in Clinical Psychology from the California Institute of Integral Studies (San Francisco). Dr. Denise is certified as a sexologist through the American College of Sexologists. She was in the first cohort to graduate from the Center for Psychedelic Therapies and Research (CPTR) at CIIS and provides psychedelic integration individually and in group settings, utilizing trauma-informed and somatics approaches. She has studied embodied spiritual practices nationally and internationally through research and experiential learning and has conducted and published research on embodied psycho-spirituality.

Diána Bósa lives and works in Hungary yet writes mainly in English. One of her plays was performed in the RS9 theatre in 2012, Budapest. Her poems became published in *Cosmic Orgasm's HURT* (Stuttgart, 2019), *Beyond Words Magazine* (Berlin, 2021), and Poetry Soup's second anthology, *PS: It's Still Poetry* (2022).

In her younger days, **Erika Lopp** chose a path to help others. She attended college and received a Bachelor of Arts in Sociology and later a Master's in Education and Counseling Psychology in order to help victims of domestic violence. Later, her heart led her to an Anthropology degree out of her love for history, archaeology, and cultural studies. She currently works for a cultural resource management firm called Corn Island Archaeology. Her passions include an avid love for the realm of magic, including mythology, magical herbalism, and moon lore. Her creative soul has led to a love for gardening, healing herbs, arts, crafts, baking, photography, and writing. Things that inspire Erika: An open moonflower at dusk, the sunrise on a cool fall morning, and the distant call of the crow.

Francesca Gentille is a Certified Clinical Sexologist, Relationship Counselor, Radio Host, award winning author, and expert in the use of BDSM and Tantra as therapeutic modalities. Priestess Francesca has been leading group ritual in Temples of Love, Sacred Eros, Sensual Healing, Divine Connection, Ritual Theatre, Tantric Kink, the Sacred Primal, the Hidden Self, and Healing for over 30 years. Her new *Certification is The Tantric Shamanic Somatic Healer Training*. She is a contributing author to the *Marriage of Sex & Spirit, Pop Goes the Witch*, and *Circles and Ceremonies, and Scry of Lust*. A quoted expert in *Rites of Pleasure*.

Hanna Verge, M.S., LPC is a thirty-two-year-old licensed practicing mental counselor, who resides on the New Jersey shore. Hanna is the mother of two children, one little boy on this earth, and one little girl who has become her teacher on the other side. She is married to Derek, whom she has known since they were thirteen and fourteen years old. In the autumn of 2022, they will be celebrating twelve years together as couple and seven years married. Their son will be six and their daughter would have turned three.

She enjoys moving and using her body, to keep the energy flowing and strong, through walks, biking, yoga, strength training, maintaining her household, and dancing and playing with her son and family. Additionally, she loves training and exercising her mind, through reading, writing, meditating, watching good movies and shows, and being overall curious and excited to learn new things.

Jaclyn Cherie is a practitioner of various forms of Folk Magick & Traditional Witchcraft. Her Catholic + Protestant upbringing mixed with lineage-based traditions are paramount in her personal practice. Ancestral Veneration through decolonization, Shadow Work, and Generational Cursebreaking.

From Appalachian Folk Magick, Slavic Witchcraft, Hekatean Witchcraft, to Luciferianism, her Craft is like a quilt; stitched together in beautiful patchwork patterns are the people, experiences, Deities and Spirits that shaped her.

Currently, Jaclyn is getting certified in Ashtanga Yoga and Kundalini Yoga as a 500HR RYT, CYT. She is also certifying as a 500HR CMT and 800HR Yoga Therapist. As a Shaivite Hindu, this was a natural progression of her journey.

A disabled, Neurodivergent, small business owner, she's kept busy adorning and blessing the world with her signature Wearable Magick™ Handcrafted Creations and otherworldly Herbal Offerings.

Jen Abha believes wholeheartedly in practicing fierce love. She continues to hone her skills as a Somatic Educator practicing Trauma Informed Care, as she calls upon intentional disciplines all leading us back to the root of our intuition. She seeks to teach from a place of dignified empowerment, and compassionate understanding. She is a believer in matrilineal ways of living and loving through her attached Mothering, embodying authenticity and truth. Passionate about cultivating growth mindsets, and building healthy relationships by doing the inner work, being asked for the collective to support our community and our Great Mother. Embodying all to walk the high road of loving boundaries, interconnected, and connected through the divine line.

May we all live a life of Love, Light and Levity – infinitely. In her name.

Originally from Fresno, CA, now living in CO, **Jenn Martinez** is a graduate of CSU Fresno with a B.A. in fine art. She is a magickal practitioner and tarot reader. Many of her drawings are inspired by meditation and visualizations during her practices as well as living life as a newly realized ADHD mom, wife, reconnecting Native American, and displaced Gen Xer. Currently her work embodies how she is attempting to balance the feelings of trying to fit into a space but still just feeling wild. The juxtaposition of spiritual and mundane duality in modern life. Ultimately most of her artwork is self-portrait in one way or another always representative of her current state of mind.

Born in India, settled in England, **Jonita D'souza** is a Feminine Lifestylist, an Author and Creatress of Exploring Femininity Ltd., assisting modern day busy women who struggle with burn-out, overwhelm and body love to reconnect with their feminine and sensual energy using the ancient Taoist and Tantric arts, so that they can create a lifestyle that is fulfilling, nurturing and pleasurable. Jonita is also a Certified Life Coach, NLP Practitioner, Master Hypnotherapist and combines the teachings of Indian feminine mysticism and shamanism in her work, facilitating monthly moon circles, online workshops, and sacred feminine retreats.

Julie A. Dickson is a poet who addresses issues including bullying, animal and human rights, nature and environment. She advocates for captive elephants and has volunteered with feral cat rescue. Her poetry appears in many journals such as Blue Heron, Misfit, Ekphrastic Review and Deadbeat Poets. Dickson holds a BPS in Behavioral Science and works in-home with seniors.

Kat Shaw prides herself on breaking through the stereotypical views of beauty that have been cast upon society by the media, having made her name painting the glorious reality that is a woman's body.

Her nude studies of real women garnered unprecedented popularity within only a few short months, as women were crying out for themselves to be portrayed in art, rather than the airbrushed images of the perfection of the female form that are so rife in today's culture.

After graduating with a fine art degree, Kat achieved a successful full-time teaching career for 14 years, and continues to teach art part-time whilst passionately pursuing her mission of world domination by empowering as many women as possible to reach their fullest potential by embracing their bodies and loving themselves wholeheartedly.

Kat spreads her inspirational magic through her artwork, her Wellbeing business "Fabulously Imperfect", and her dedication to Goddess energy.

Reiki is a huge part of her life, and as a Reiki Master, Kat is committed to sharing Reiki, teaching Usui, Angelic and Karuna Reiki, and channelling Reiki energy through her artwork to uplift and heal.

As a Sister of Avalon, Kat also works directly with her Goddess consciousness, connecting to Goddess and Priestess energy and translating it into Divine Feminine infused paintings to inspire women and spread Goddess love.

Kat is also mum to a gorgeous teenage daughter, a bellydancer and an avid pioneer to improve the lives of rescue animals.

Kay Louise Aldred is a researcher, writer, and educator, who catalyses individual, institutional and collective evolution – through education, embodiment, and creativity – amalgamating metacognition, intuition, and instinct.

She has published three workbooks of her own with Girl God Books – *Mentorship of Goddess: Growing Sacred Womanhood, Making Love with the Divine: Sacred, Ecstatic, Erotic Experiences* and *Somatic Shamanism: Your Fleshy Knowing as the Tree of Life* – in addition to co-authoring *Embodied Education: Creating Safe Space for Learning Facilitating and Sharing* with her husband Dan Aldred. The couple reside in North Yorkshire, England.

www.kaylouisealdred.com
Instagram, Twitter, and LinkedIn @kaylouisealdred

Lauren Raine, MFA, has been creating visual and performance art about the Great Mother since the early 80's. She studied sacred mask traditions in Bali, and exhibited at Buka Creati Gallery in Ubud, Bali. Her collection of "contemporary temple masks" devoted to worldwide stories of the sacred feminine, The Masks of the Goddess, traveled throughout the U.S. for over 20 years used by dancers, ritualists and storytellers, and venues including the Chapel of Sacred Mirrors, the International Mask Symposium, the New College of California, and the Parliament of World Religions. In 2007 she received a Fellowship with the Alden Dow Creativity Center at Northwood University and a Puffin Grant for her "Spider Woman" Community Arts Project. In 2009 she was resident artist at the Henry Luce Center for the Arts at Wesley Theological Seminary in Washington, DC. Currently she works in ceramic sculpture and teaches at the Tucson Clay Co-op. www.laurenraine.com / www.masksofthegoddess.com

Lily Munroe is an Australian devotee of the Goddess, writer, artist, oracle, witch of olde, priestess path walker in many lives, and women's liberationist.

Louise Cox is an artist and writer. Seeking to understand her extra sensory nature from an early age. She has studied the occult, shamanism and has a degree in Theology specialising in Classical and Tantric Yoga. Currently she is re-engaging with her magical nature, chronicling this through writing "The Forgotten Magic" on The Nephilim Rising blog.

Dr Lynne Sedgmore CBE is a Priestess of Avalon, poetess, coach, and non-executive board member   living in Glastonbury UK. She is the founder and author of the *Goddess Luminary Leadership Wheel* book and trainings, and author of *Presence, A Profound Antidote to Climate Anxiety.*

Her three poetry collections include *Enlivenment, Healing through the Goddess,* and *Crone Times.* Her poems and articles have been published in an international range of publications, including several Girl God anthologies. She is regularly interviewed on podcasts about her work. Lynne is a mother, stepmother, and grandmother of two teenagers. In 2016 she was named one of the UK's 100 Women of Spirit.

Michelle Moirai is a digital artist who lives and works in Morgantown, West Virginia. Her personal style focuses on duplication of traditional art mediums in a digital setting, and the themes of transformation and uncovering what has been hidden. Currently, Moirai works as the Assistant Director of Marketing Technology for the Benjamin M. Statler College of Engineering and Mineral Resources at West Virginia University, where she uses her design talents to create websites for the college. Outside of work, she continues to create digital paintings, and is currently exploring how text-to-art artificial intelligence can be beneficial to the advancement of the digital arts.

https://mementomoirai.com/

Molly Remer, MSW, D.Min, is a priestess facilitating women's circles, seasonal rituals, and family ceremonies in central Missouri. Molly and her husband Mark co-create Story Goddesses at Brigid's Grove. Molly is the author of nine books, including *Walking with Persephone, Whole and Holy, Womanrunes,* and the *Goddess Devotional.* She is the creator of the devotional experience #30DaysofGoddess and she loves savoring small magic and everyday enchantment.

Nuit Moore is a ceremonial creatrix, ritual artist, witch, and eco-feminist activist whose work has served the return of the Goddess to the collective consciousness. As priestess, she has been teaching and offering women's ceremonies for 30 years. Nuit has been a visionary voice and red thread weaver of the Blood Mysteries and an activist of the eco-menstruation movement since 1991. Much of her path is rooted in women's rites/rights, which is also embodied in her work as a Wise Woman herbalist. Currently, Nuit is embracing the alchemy of her 50's and is excited to be on the journey. She is currently directing her focus more deeply to her work as a creatrix and ritual artist of multiple forms, to her ancestral lineages, as well as towards an evolving and expanded service to Dea Madre.

She can be found on Instagram @nuitmoore and her herbal and ritual arts offerings can be found at www.terratemplearts.etsy.com.

Pat Daly (editor) is a mother of three daughters and proud grandma. A published author / writer on career and job search issues, Pat lives in Portland, Oregon. She has edited all the Girl God Books from the beginning.

Ramona Chalmers is an emerging poet and writer based in the Eastern Cape, South Africa. Her love affair with words started at a very young age, where she devoured books and wrote poetry as a means to make sense of her world. Her poetry touches on the fragility and strength of the human spirit, our inner emotional landscape, and themes of struggle, transformation, and rebirth. She joined a creative writing class hosted by the Emonti Writers Circle in 2019 and this journey culminated in helping her find her voice and compiling her first collection of poetry, to be published in 2023. Her heart song poem *Warrior* was awarded a gold certificate in 2019.

Her second volume of poetry, *Nirvana*, is currently in the making as she transitions into becoming a full-time poet and writer. Her hobbies include reading, meditative walking, yoga and exploring new places, people, food, and culture.

Rhonda Melanson is a poet and teacher living in Sarnia, Ontario Canada. She recently published a chapbook on Mother Mary called *My Name is Mary* (Alien Buddha Press).

Sarah K. Grundy, an author writing her first novel, *MORGAN*, while working as a writer for sustainable beauty.

Miss **Shalini Persaud** lives in Guyana, South America and has always been interested in Dark Divine Feminine deities from early in her twenties, despite following different spiritual paths before. Born on July 5, 1968, her open mind and willingness to be authentic and outspoken has allowed her insight into many aspects of spirituality. She lives alone with four cats and feeds the feral cats and a few homeless dogs in her afternoons, while being engaged in a work-from-home job during the week. As a Human Resources specialist, her insight and understanding of the human psyche and psychology has also helped in her ability to be approachable and empathetic to persons. Shalini has written several unpublished pieces of poetry, most of which revolve around dark themes and is also an English and Spanish tutor, with a B.A. in English Literature and Spanish and Diplomas in Personnel Management, HR Management and Banking & Finance.

Sharyn Ginyard is a professional R & B oldies singer and producer living in Philadelphia, Pennsylvania, as well as a mother, grandmother who still works. She is a student of kundalini yoga who has completed training as an emergence priestess under the mentorship of Elisha Halpin in the heroine's mystical journey and Embodied the Community programs.

Sionainn McLean is a polytheist fire witch and animist, on a crazy spiritual journey over the last 25 years. She is a priestess of The Morrigan and has served the Great Queen for over 5 years. A recent graduate of the Community Ministry program with Cherry Hill Seminary, she is also working towards her spiritual direction certificate. She is the owner and operator of Liminal Raven Ministries whose mission is to aid in self-empowerment, provide inspiration, guidance, support, and ministry to pagans as well as to nurture spiritual growth in others. She's also a mom, wife, writer, painter, and gardener.

Sonee Singh is a cross-cultural seeker of deep knowing. She writes stories of self-discovery to encourage people to accept themselves for who they are and live life on their own terms. Her tales are of her character's definitive moments on their life's journey. The mystical and spiritual are integral in her storytelling, as is her multi-cultural background.

Sonee is of Indian descent, born in Mexico, raised in Colombia, and resides in the United States. When not traveling, reading, or writing, she indulges in meditation, yoga, and aromatherapy.

Sonee has been published in two anthologies: *Blessing the Page* and *The Colours of Me*. Her first novel was published in 2022. She published three books in her Soul-Seeker collection of poetry: *Embody*, *Embrace* and *Embolden*.

Stella Tomlinson is an author, poet, and Priestess.

Her work explores belonging, emotional wellbeing and self-worth through a lens of the seasonal wisdom of nature spirituality; conscious menstruation and menopause; and deconditioning from patriarchy.

Her offerings are based on over twenty years' experience in personal and spiritual healing and development through meditation, yoga, mindfulness, energy healing, menstrual cycle awareness, and Goddess and nature spirituality, and she's been teaching and writing in these fields since 2011.

Tamara Albanna has always been connected to the Goddess, even when she didn't realize it. As a Doula and Childbirth Educator, she witnessed divinity first-hand through other women. Now as a writer, artist, Reiki healer and Tarot reader, she hopes to help others overcome their difficult pasts while healing with the Divine Mother. She has published two books on *Inanna—Inanna's Ascent: Reclaiming Female Power* (co-edited with Trista Hendren and Pat Daly) and *My Name is Inanna*; two books on Willendorf— *Willendorf's Legacy: The Sacred Body* (co-edited with Trista Hendren and Pat Daly) and *My Name is Goddess of Willendorf*—as well as four poetry chapbooks, *As I Lay By the Tigris and Weep, Rosewater, Kismet,* and *Kissing the Moon.* Tamara currently resides in Europe with her family. Website: https://tamara-albanna.com.

Tara Greene, High Priestess, natural born Psychic remembers her past lives and multi-dimensional origins. Internationally renowned Canadian Tarot Reader, Astrologer, women's spirituality, Dreamwork, workshop leader, lipstick reader for Gucci, Estee Lauder, Bite Beauty. A trained artist and Transformational Psychotherapist, Tara has enlightened 30,000+ people since 1991. She accurately predicts elections, sports, celebrities, and a famous Tweet of Duchess Meghan going into labor 12 hours before. She writes Horoscopes daily on her blog, for Moonology, The Cosmic Intelligence Agency and Tim Horton's.

A passionate natural birthing advocate, she has two beautiful children born at home with midwives in 1983 and 1996 and is a proud Crone grandmother.

A double Sagittarius, Scorpio Rising, loves to travel; visiting sacred sites: Egypt Stonehenge, Ephesus, Timbuktu, Guatemala, and Mexico. She lives in Toronto with her artist husband, a wild kitten, canary, their daughter, but Sedona is her spiritual home. "Remember who you really are." She advises.

Trista Hendren founded Girl God Books in 2011 to support a necessary unraveling of the patriarchal worldview of divinity. Her first book—*The Girl God*, a children's picture book—was a response to her own daughter's inability to see herself reflected in the divine. Since then, she has published more than 50 books with hundreds of contributors from across the globe. Originally from Portland, Oregon, she now lives in Bergen, Norway. You can learn more about her projects at www.thegirlgod.com.

Wakanda Rose is a Priestess of the Goddess, a Tradition Keeper of the Ancient Ways, a Medicine Woman, a Creative Artist, and a Musician. She blends Science and Metaphysics together to bring back to life the way of the Goddess. She feels a part of her time on Earth is to walk in others' darkness and trauma, bringing the Medicine of Hope + Self-Empowerment and being a support to come back to Divine Unity and the Sacred Goddess way if they so choose. She is an ally to the Plant World with seeing these beings as sacred sentient energy and honours the Herbal Medicine path. Wakanda Rose blends many paths together, honouring each tradition and culture that she gets to experience to re-empower herself and others – and walk the path of the Goddess and Unity.

Ara's Acknowledgments

I would like to acknowledge my co-editors Trista Hendren, Jaclyn Cherie, and Pat Daly for their tireless dedication to this powerful project. Collaborating with *Girl God Books* has been an absolute dream come true for me and it was amazing being part of this team. Thank you, sisters, for your support, patience, and guidance.

I want to acknowledge the wonderful contributors of this anthology for sharing their inspirational writing and illustrations. Thank you to Kat Shaw for her stunning cover art. Thank you to my readers and all those who resonated with my work at *The Goddess Circle* over the last decade. I appreciate you all.

I want to thank my family for their continued support and love. And to my dog Sonny, my bestest little buddy and darling fluff pup, who was always by my side lovingly each day, and now watches eternally over me from the stars. Mama loves and misses you always and forever, sweet boy.

Until we meet again.

C. Ara Campbell

Jaclyn's Acknowledgments

I would like to acknowledge, first and foremost, Trista Hendren, the owner of Girl God Books, and one of my co-editors and dearest friends. Her belief in me and my talent gives me wings. I was honored to work with my beloved sister and co-editor, Ara Campbell, on this project as well. Bows of gratitude to all the women, Femmes, and artists that helped bring this book, this dream to life. Neverending love and appreciation to my partner who believes in my dreams often more than I do. His encouragement, his strength, and his silliness get me through my most wild, creative days. Lastly, I would like to thank my mother, who cheers me on the loudest. She believed in me, my daydreams and aspirations long before I grasped they could be real. We have walked side by side through life for my entire life and many past ones. Deepest gratitude to the powerhouse that created me. Because of her, my fire burns eternal.

Thank you. Thank you. Thank you.

Trista's Acknowledgments

I would like to acknowledge my co-editors. My mother, **Pat Daly**, has edited each and every one of my books. There would be no Girl God Books without her enormous contributions. I was thrilled to work with my beloved Sisters, **Ara Campbell** and **Jaclyn Cherie**, on this project as well.

Tremendous gratitude to **Kat Shaw** for allowing us to feature her gorgeous painting as the cover art.

Enormous appreciation to my husband **Anders Løberg**, who prepared the document for printing and helped with website updates. Your love, support and many contributions made this book possible.

Lastly, I would like to thank my dear sisters **Tamara Albanna, Susan Morgaine, Jeanette Bjørnsen, Camilla Berge Wolff, Kay Louise Aldred, Sharon Smith, Arlene Bailey, Arna Baartz, Kat Shaw**, and **Alyscia Cunningham** for always being right there to cheer me on in the spirit of true sisterhood.

Thank you to all our readers and Girl God supporters over the years. We love and appreciate you!

If you enjoyed this book, please consider writing a brief review on Amazon and/or Goodreads.

What's Next?!

Kali Ma: the Dark Mother – Edited by C. Ara Campbell, Jaclyn Cherie, Pat Daly and Trista Hendren

Wounded Feminine: Grieving with Goddess – Edited by Claire Dorey, Trista Hendren, and Pat Daly

Sacred Breasts: an Inspirational Anthology for Living Your Breast Life – Edited by Barbara O'Meara, Trista Hendren and Pat Daly

Cerridwen and the Cauldron: a Celtic Tale of Magic – a children's book by Emma Clark, illustrated by Reti Toriella

The Wisdom of Cerridwen: Transforming in Her Cosmic Brew – Edited by Emma Clark, Trista Hendren, and Pat Daly

Lady of the Forge: Stories and Art Dedicated to the Goddess Brigid – Edited by Isca Johnson, Trista Hendren, and Pat Daly

Goddess Chants and Songs Book – Edited by Trista Hendren and Pat Daly

And Still, I Rise – Kat Shaw

Anthologies and children's books on Asherah, Cerridwen, the Black Madonna, Mary Magdalene, Mother Mary, Aradia, Spider Woman, Persephone, and Hecate are also in the works.

http://thegirlgod.com/publishing.php

Made in United States
Cleveland, OH
04 May 2025

16663383R00116